BestMasters

Mit **„BestMasters“** zeichnet Springer die besten Masterarbeiten aus, die an renommierten Hochschulen in Deutschland, Österreich und der Schweiz entstanden sind. Die mit Höchstnote ausgezeichneten Arbeiten wurden durch Gutachter zur Veröffentlichung empfohlen und behandeln aktuelle Themen aus unterschiedlichen Fachgebieten der Naturwissenschaften, Psychologie, Sozialwissenschaften, Technik und Wirtschaftswissenschaften. Die Reihe wendet sich an Praktiker und Wissenschaftler gleichermaßen und soll insbesondere auch Nachwuchswissenschaftlern Orientierung geben.

Springer awards **“BestMasters”** to the best master’s theses which have been completed at renowned Universities in Germany, Austria, and Switzerland. The studies received highest marks and were recommended for publication by supervisors. They address current issues from various fields of research in natural sciences, psychology, social sciences, technology, and economics. The series addresses practitioners as well as scientists and, in particular, offers guidance for early stage researchers.

R.M. Vajirapanie Bandaranayake

The Differential Impact of Investor Behavioural Biases on US Sustainable and Non-Sustainable Firms

A Three-Factor Model Approach

Springer Gabler

R.M. Vajirapanie Bandaranayake
Department 1 Economics
HWR Berlin
Berlin, Germany

ISSN 2625-3577 ISSN 2625-3615 (electronic)
BestMasters
ISBN 978-3-658-50667-4 ISBN 978-3-658-50668-1 (eBook)
https://doi.org/10.1007/978-3-658-50668-1

This Springer Gabler imprint is published by the registered company Springer Fachmedien Wiesbaden GmbH, part of Springer Nature.
The registered company address is: Abraham-Lincoln-Str. 46, 65189 Wiesbaden, Germany

Foreword

The motivation for this thesis stems from a growing personal and academic interest in the intersection of sustainability and behavioural finance, two fields that are shaping the future of investment decision-making. Throughout my studies, I became increasingly curious about how cognitive biases influence financial markets, especially in the context of firms committed to ESG principles. This work aims to contribute to the ongoing discussion on the relevance of behavioural factors in explaining price anomalies between leaders and laggards in terms of sustainability.

I would like to express my sincere gratitude to my supervisors, Prof. Dr. Natalie Packham and Marwin Heinemann, M.A., for their support and insightful feedback throughout this process.

Berlin
January 2025

Abstract

This study explores how investor behavioural biases influence sustainable (high-ESG) and non-sustainable (low-ESG) firms in the United States, using the behavioural three-factor model introduced by Daniel, Hirshleifer, and Sun (2020). The model includes two behavioural factors: limited attention bias, which captures short-term anomalies (indicated by the Post-Earnings Announcement Drift or PEAD), and overconfidence bias, a long-term bias (as indicated by the Financing or FIN factor). By analyzing both high- and low-ESG portfolios, the study finds that both portfolios are exposed to the two biases, but the degree of exposure varies significantly. The high-ESG portfolio shows positive loadings on both behavioural factors, indicating efficient price corrections, while the low-ESG portfolio sees negative loadings. This difference in factor loadings for ESG portfolios is novel. It is likely due to arbitrage frictions. The study also finds that these biases are more pronounced during bull market phases, while they diminish in bear market phases (the overconfidence bias weakens, and the limited attention bias loses statistical significance). Furthermore, the high-ESG portfolio returns are less susceptible to overall market movements and thus offer greater downside protection during bear markets.

Contents

Abbreviations

AMEX	American Stock Exchange
CAPM	Capital Asset Pricing Model
CAR	Cumulative Abnormal Returns
CRSP	Center for Research in Security Prices
CSI	Composite Share Issuance
EMH	Efficient Market Hypothesis
ESG	Environmental, Social, and Governance
EU	European Union
FIN	Financing Factor
GRI	Global Reporting Initiative
HML	High Minus Low
IFRS	International Financial Reporting Standards
IFRS S1	IFRS Sustainability Reporting Disclosure Standard
IFRS S2	IFRS Climate-Related Disclosure Standard
NASDAQ	National Association of Securities Dealers Automated Quotations
NSI	Net Share Issuance
NYSE	New York Stock Exchange
PEAD	Post-Earnings Announcement Drift
S&P	500 Index—Standard and Poor's 500 Index
SMB	Small Minus Big
SRI	Sustainable and Responsible Investment
SUE	Standardized Unexpected Earnings
US	United States
USD	United States Dollar

List of Tables

1 Introduction

In the 1970s, the efficient markets theory reached its peak, aligning perfectly with the rational expectations revolution in economic theory (Shiller, 2003, p. 1). During this period, it was widely accepted that speculative asset prices, like stock prices, reflected all available information about their fundamental values, changing only in response to new, sensible information. This idea, which tied financial markets to economic fundamentals through rational expectations, became a dominant theoretical framework in finance (Shiller, 2003, p. 1).

Behavioural finance emerged as a response to the traditional assumptions of rationality in classical finance models (Shiller, 2003, p. 1). It incorporates insights from psychology and social science to understand better how people make decisions in financial markets. Unlike classical economic theories, which assume fully rational agents with perfect computational abilities, behavioural finance recognizes that human decision-making is often influenced by cognitive biases, emotions, and psychological limitations (Mullainathan and Thaler, 2000).

In academic literature, many behavioural biases have been identified. In this study, we mainly explore overconfidence bias and limited attention bias. Overconfidence bias, as described by Barberis, Shleifer and Vishny (1998), occurs when investors overestimate their ability to assess information and make predictions about future market movements. This leads to excessive trading and mispricing, as investors place too much weight on private information while underreacting to public signals. Daniel, Hirshleifer and Subrahmanyam (1998) further explored this and found that overconfidence leads to momentum effects in the short term and price reversals in the long term.

On the other hand, limited attention bias occurs when investors fail to incorporate new information into stock prices fully. This is particularly evident in

R.M. V. Bandaranayake, *The Differential Impact of Investor Behavioural Biases on US Sustainable and Non-Sustainable Firms*, BestMasters,
https://doi.org/10.1007/978-3-658-50668-1_1

the post-earnings announcement period, where stock prices tend to adjust gradually rather than immediately, leading to sustained price drifts (Foster, Olsen and Shevlin, 1984). Studies by Hirshleifer, Lim and Teoh (2009) and DellaVigna and Pollet (2009) have shown that limited attention is more pronounced when investors are distracted by other events, such as multiple earnings announcements, market news, or the Friday effect.

Sustainable investing, which integrates ESG factors into investment decision-making, has seen significant growth in recent years. According to Ciciretti, Dalò, and Ferri (2023, p. 3), the sustainable and responsible investment (SRI) market is projected to reach USD 35 trillion by 2025. While there is substantial empirical research on ESG investing and asset prices, the literature on ESG investing and behavioural biases remains relatively scarce. This research intends to fill that gap by exploring the degree of influence of behavioural biases such as overconfidence bias and limited attention bias on high-ESG (ESG leaders) and low-ESG (ESG laggards) firms in the US.

The primary research question addressed by this study is: how, and to what extent, do overconfidence and limited attention biases influence the returns of high-ESG and low-ESG firms in the US? The study is motivated by the recent research by Badía, Goicoechea and Ugarte (2024), who found that high-ESG firms in the EU are not exposed to overconfidence and limited attention bias, whereas low-ESG firms in the EU are only exposed to overconfidence bias. This study investigates whether similar patterns exist in the US or if the nature of ESG investing in the US results in different anomaly outcomes.

The study is built on the behavioural three-factor model introduced by Daniel, Hirshleifer and Sun (2020), and it is the same theoretical and methodological framework followed by Badía, Goicoechea, and Ugarte (2024) in their EU study. The model incorporates two behavioural factors: Post-Earnings Announcement Drift (PEAD) and Financing Factor (FIN Factor), alongside the traditional market factor from the Capital Asset Pricing Model (CAPM). The PEAD factor captures short-term mispricing resulting from investor underreaction to earnings surprises, while the FIN factor captures long-term mispricing driven by corporate financing decisions, such as equity issuances or share repurchases.

The study uses a combination of empirical data and theoretical analysis to investigate these questions. The dataset includes nearly 1,400 publicly listed firms in the US, focusing on firms that have ESG scores in the Thomson Reuters Refinitiv database. The data spans nearly two decades, from June 2005 to June 2023, providing a comprehensive view of how behavioural biases have impacted ESG leaders and laggards over time. The study uses a binary classification approach to distinguish between high-ESG (top 10%) and low-ESG (bottom 10%) firms using a dummy variable (1 = high-ESG, 0 = low-ESG). It then applies the behavioural three-factor model to analyze the impact of PEAD and FIN on both high- and low-ESG portfolios.

The regression results suggest that both high-ESG and low-ESG firms in the US are exposed to overconfidence and limited attention biases, but the degree of impact varies. High-ESG firms show positive loadings on both the PEAD and FIN factors, indicating that they experience more efficient price corrections. In contrast, low-ESG firms exhibit negative loadings on these factors, suggesting that they suffer from persistent mispricing, likely due to higher arbitrage frictions. This finding is novel. Moreover, high-ESG firms also show less sensitivity to overall market fluctuations, providing better downside protection. The findings suggest that high-ESG firms are better positioned for risk mitigation and offer predictable future returns due to more efficient price corrections.

The findings from the US and EU reveal key differences in how behavioural biases impact high- and low-ESG portfolios. In the EU, high-ESG firms are not exposed to overconfidence and limited attention biases, as evidenced by the lack of statistical significance for the PEAD and FIN factors. In contrast, low-ESG firms in the EU are only exposed to the overconfidence bias (Badía, Goicoechea, and Ugarte, 2024). Meanwhile, both high- and low-ESG firms in the US are affected by both biases. The difference in findings between the US (author research) and the EU (Badía, Goicoechea, and Ugarte, 2024) is intriguing, given that both studies used the same theoretical and methodological framework to test the identical biases across two developed capital markets.

Badía, Goicoechea, and Ugarte (2024) do not investigate why EU high-ESG firms are resistant to overconfidence and limited attention biases. However, there are several supporting arguments in the literature. D'Apice and Ferri (2021), along with Ciciretti, Dalò, and Ferri (2023), find that higher ESG ratings in the EU, compared to those in the US, result from stricter ESG disclosure regulations. Additionally, European firms place a cultural emphasis on sustainability (Beloe, 2016). These factors likely contribute to the lower mispricing observed among European ESG leaders. However, some opposing evidence also exists. LaBella et al. (2019) find that ESG ratings are subject to size and region biases, and therefore, larger European firms tend to have higher average ESG scores compared to their US counterparts. The size bias (Drempetic, Klein and Zwergel, 2020; Giese et al., 2019) and the EU's regional bias (Doyle, 2018) have also been confirmed in other studies. Moreover, recent research by Gavrilakis and Floros (2024) found that European ESG leaders exhibit herding behaviour, which further complicates the EU findings. As such, the empirical evidence suggesting that high-ESG firms in the EU are insulated from overconfidence and limited attention biases (Badía, Goicoechea, and Ugarte, 2024) may warrant further research.

The study also examines how overconfidence and limited attention biases impact US ESG leaders and laggards during volatile market conditions (bull and bear markets). During bull markets, both high- and low-ESG portfolios show increased exposure to overconfidence and limited attention biases, with higher coefficients for PEAD and FIN. This aligns with prior studies suggesting that overconfidence drives excessive trading in bull markets (Gervais and Odean, 2001; Chuang and Lee, 2006). In contrast, during bear markets, these biases taper off, with PEAD losing statistical significance and the FIN factor weakening. This reflects lower investor optimism and increased risk aversion (Hou, Peng, and Xiong, 2008). Additionally, high-ESG portfolios provide downside protection during bear markets, as the Market Returns factor loses significance, suggesting that investors seek refuge in sustainable firms during down markets (Nofsinger and Varma, 2012). This behaviour aligns with prospect theory (Kahneman and Tversky, 1979; Nofsinger and Varma, 2012).

One of the key limitations of this study is the reliance on ESG data from a single provider, Refinitiv, which may introduce biases related to size, region, and industry (LaBella et al., 2019; Drempetic, Klein and Zwergel, 2020; Giese et al., 2019; Doyle, 2018). Future research could address these limitations by incorporating data from multiple rating providers and considering industry-specific factors. Regarding future research directions, there are two main suggestions. First, the study's findings regarding the differences in factor loadings for high- and low-ESG portfolios across market phases present a potential avenue for further research. Investigating the role of arbitrage frictions, which are higher for stocks with lower liquidity, higher idiosyncratic risk and low institutional participation, could help explain these differences (Kumar and Lee, 2006). Second, the observed regional differences in behavioural biases between high-ESG firms in the EU and the US may be attributed to regulatory and cultural differences or rating biases, which could be further explored. Additionally, it would be interesting to examine how evolving ESG regulations and the global harmonization of sustainability standards (such as IFRS sustainability standards) help bridge the regional gap in behavioural biases. Furthermore, while the behavioural three-factor model applied in this study highlights statistically significant effects from PEAD and FIN factors, their added value beyond the traditional market factor appears limited. The relatively small increase in explanatory power suggests that, although behaviourally motivated, these factors contribute marginally to explaining return variation within the current model framework.

Overall, this paper makes several contributions. First, it provides empirical evidence that, in the US, even ESG leaders are exposed to overconfidence and limited attention biases, just as ESG laggards are. Second, the difference in factor loadings (both negative and positive) between high- and low-ESG firms indicates that low-ESG firms are exposed to high arbitrage frictions and, therefore, subjected to persistent mispricing. In contrast, high-ESG firms experience more efficient corrections of anomalies. Third, behavioural biases become more pronounced during bull market phases. In contrast, during bear market phases, the overconfidence bias weakens, and the limited attention bias does not exist (no statistical significance). Fourth, high-ESG portfolios are less susceptible to overall market movements and offer greater downside protection during bear market phases.

The remainder of this paper is structured as follows: Chapter 2 provides the literature review, and Chap. 3 presents the research methodology. Chapter 4 discusses the results. Finally, Chapter 5 provides limitations and future research opportunities, and Chap. 6 concludes the paper.

Literature Review 2

In this chapter, the theoretical framework of this study will be established. First, the evolution of behavioural finance will be discussed, followed by a discussion on theories of overconfidence and limited attention bias. Next, the behavioural three-factor model introduced by Daniel, Hirshleifer, and Lin (2020) will be examined, given its significance for this study. The role of behavioural biases during bull and bear markets will then be explored. Next, the intersection of behavioural finance and sustainable finance will be analyzed, given its relevance for this study. This will include a look at behavioural biases in sustainability investments, the EU-US ESG region bias and empirical evidence on the performance of sustainability-focused funds during volatile market conditions.

2.1 Evolution of Behavioural Finance

The evolution of financial theory over the last half-century is characterized by two major revolutions. The first is the neoclassical revolution in finance, which originated in the 1960s with the development of the Capital Asset Pricing Model (CAPM) and the Efficient Market Hypothesis (EMH), and continued into the 1970s with the introduction of the intertemporal CAPM and arbitrage-based option pricing models (Shiller, 2006). The second major shift in financial theory is the behavioural revolution, which emerged in the 1980s. Behavioural finance focuses on understanding the reasons behind market volatility, identifying various anomalies, and incorporating insights from psychological theories into asset pricing (Shiller, 2006).

The Prospect Theory, introduced by Kahneman and Tversky (1979), laid the foundation for Behavioural Finance (Curtis, 2004). Their research showed that

R.M. V. Bandaranayake, *The Differential Impact of Investor Behavioural Biases on US Sustainable and Non-Sustainable Firms*, BestMasters,
https://doi.org/10.1007/978-3-658-50668-1_2

individuals often deviate from traditional utility models due to cognitive biases. The study highlights key behavioural concepts such as the certainty effect, where people prefer guaranteed outcomes over uncertain ones, and loss aversion, which explains why individuals tend to fear losses more than they value equivalent gains (Kahneman and Tversky, 1979). Building on Prospect Theory, a year later, Thaler (1980) introduced key behavioural concepts such as the endowment effect (where individuals tend to overvalue items they own) and the sunk cost fallacy (where past expenses irrationally influence future decisions).

These findings led academics to challenge the long-standing assumption that investors are always rational and instead suggest that real-world investors often display "quasi-rational behaviour" (Thaler, 1999, p. 4). Many questioned the excess volatility seen in the market, and some argued that such volatility could be driven by irrational factors, such as "sunspots", "animal spirits", or just mass psychology (Shiller, 2003, p. 2). As elegantly stated by Statman (1995, p. 21), "people in standard finance are rational. They are not confused by frames, they are not affected by cognitive errors, they do not know the pain of regret, and they have no lapses of self-control. People in behavioural finance may not always be rational, but they are always normal".

This next section will have a brief look at two key behavioural biases: limited attention bias and overconfidence bias, which have been extensively studied for their impact on asset pricing and market anomalies. These two biases are also central to the present study.

2.2 Overconfidence Bias

Bondt and Thaler (1995, p. 5) said that overconfidence bias is the most well-documented cognitive bias in the psychology of judgment. They explained that individuals often overestimate the accuracy and reliability of their knowledge, and as a result, asset prices see excessive trading and mispricing.

2.2.1 Theoretical Foundations of Overconfidence Bias

Barberis, Shleifer and Vishny (1998) introduced a parsimonious model for investor sentiment, which explained two common anomalies in financial markets: underreaction and overreaction. Their research showed that stock prices tend to underreact to news in the short term (one to twelve months) and overreact in the long term (three to five years). This pattern suggests that investors often fail to fully incorporate new information immediately, leading to momentum effects. However, as extreme valuations build up, prices eventually revert to the mean (Barberis, Shleifer and Vishny 1998). This evidence challenges the Efficient Markets Hypothesis (EMH), which assumes that prices always reflect all available information. The authors concluded that sophisticated investors (e.g., arbitrageurs) could systematically exploit these inefficiencies to earn superior returns without bearing additional risk. Unlike rational asset pricing models that link returns solely to risk factors, their model suggests that behavioural biases influence asset prices, reflecting imperfect rationality.

Building on this, Daniel, Hirshleifer and Subrahmanyam (1998) proposed that **overreaction and underreaction in security markets arise from overconfidence bias** and biased self-attribution. Overconfident investors place excessive weight on private information signals while underreacting to public signals. This behaviour leads to momentum effects in the short run, as investors continue to rely on their biased views, and long-run reversals, as market corrections set in over time (Daniel, Hirshleifer and Subrahmanyam, 1998). Their model explains key empirical asset pricing patterns, such as negative long-lag autocorrelations where overconfident investors cause excessive short-term price movements, leading to subsequent reversals[1]. Furthermore, excess volatility occurs as prices fluctuate more than justified by rational expectations due to overreaction.

An important implication of their model is that returns can be predicted based on public events. Since overconfident investors overreact to private information but underreact to public news, certain events (such as earnings announcements, stock repurchases and equity issuances) create predictable return patterns. For instance, stock repurchases are often undertaken when managers perceive their stock as undervalued, leading to superior long-term returns. Conversely, share issuances occur when firms believe their stock is overvalued, leading to future underperformance (Daniel, Hirshleifer and Subrahmanyam, 1998). This pattern aligns with their broader argument that prices overreact to private information but underreact to public signals, making corporate financing decisions useful predictors of future returns.

[1] Negative long-lag autocorrelation refers to a statistical pattern in stock returns where price movements over an extended period tend to reverse. Initially, overconfident investors drive excessive price changes, causing positive autocorrelation, where price increases (or decreases) persist for some time. However, as new public information continues to emerge, these overreactions are gradually corrected, leading to negative autocorrelation in the long run, where past price increases are followed by future declines and vice versa (Daniel, Hirshleifer and Subrahmanyam, 1998, p. 18).

2.2.2 Extending the Overconfidence Model: The 2001 Study

Daniel, Hirshleifer and Subrahmanyam (2001) refined their model by incorporating the role of arbitrageurs in responding to mispricing. While their 1998 paper primarily focused on how overconfident investors cause underreaction and overreaction, their 2001 study examined whether systematic mispricing persists in equilibrium.

One key development was the integration of both risk and mispricing measures in explaining expected stock returns. They argued that, in equilibrium, returns are influenced not only by covariance risk (as captured by the beta factor in CAPM) but also by systematic mispricing driven by overconfidence (Daniel, Hirshleifer and Subrahmanyam, 2001). This explains why fundamental-to-price ratios (e.g., book-to-market or earnings-to-price) often predict future stock returns better than beta (Daniel, Hirshleifer and Subrahmanyam, 2001).

Another contribution was a more detailed examination of arbitrageurs. Unlike classical models, where arbitrage eliminates all mispricing, they showed that risk-averse arbitrageurs correct only idiosyncratic mispricing, while systematic (market) mispricing persists due to overconfident investors.

Furthermore, they explored how overconfidence affects trading volume and volatility. Since overconfident investors overestimate their informational advantage, they engage in excessive trading, leading to higher volume and volatility. High trading volume signals strong disagreement between overconfident traders and rational arbitrageurs, which contributes to market inefficiencies (Daniel, Hirshleifer and Subrahmanyam, 2001).

2.2.3 The 2010 Extension: A Financing-Based Misvaluation Factor

Hirshleifer and Jiang (2010) extended the overconfidence literature by introducing a financing-based misvaluation factor, linking corporate financing decisions to systematic mispricing. Their study introduced the Undervalued Minus Overvalued (UMO) factor: a zero-investment portfolio[2], which takes long positions

[2] A zero-investment portfolio is a trading strategy that involves simultaneously taking long positions in one set of securities (expected winners) and short positions in another set (expected losers) without requiring an initial capital outlay. This strategy is commonly used in asset pricing models, such as the Fama-French Three-Factor Model (1996 and afterwards), to isolate systematic return patterns. The return on a zero-investment portfolio is

in repurchasing firms (which are undervalued) and short positions in issuing firms (which are overvalued). This factor was designed to capture mispricing that persists beyond standard risk-based explanations.

Hirshleifer and Jiang (2010) hypothesized that UMO factor loadings predict future returns, even for firms not actively issuing or repurchasing shares. Firms with positive UMO loadings tend to be undervalued and experience higher future returns as mispricing corrects. For instance, if investors irrationally expect oil prices to remain low, firms that benefit from higher oil prices (e.g., solar power vendors) become undervalued, repurchase shares, and load positively on UMO, while firms negatively affected by low oil prices (e.g., airlines) become overvalued, issue equity, and load negatively (Hirshleifer and Jiang, 2010). Similarly, if investor sentiment favours high-tech firms, low-tech firms become undervalued, engage in repurchases, and load positively on UMO, while overvalued high-tech firms issue equity, leading to negative UMO loadings. In both cases, positive loadings indicate undervaluation and predict higher future returns as mispricing corrects over time (Hirshleifer and Jiang, 2010).

2.2.4 Further Empirical Evidence Supporting Overconfidence Bias

Chuang and Lee (2006) tested four key implications of the overconfidence hypothesis and found that overconfident investors tend to overreact to private information but underreact to public signals. Their results showed that market gains encourage excessive trading, leading to higher volatility and greater mispricing. Overconfident investors also underestimate risk, leading them to hold riskier securities, which further contributes to price distortions (Chuang and Lee, 2006).

Scott, Stumpp and Xu (2003) examined overconfidence bias in international markets and found similar mispricing patterns across different economies, including the United States, United Kingdom, Japan, Germany, and France. Their findings showed that overconfidence bias is a global phenomenon affecting asset prices across different market structures (Scott, Stumpp and Xu, 2003).

Michailova and Schmidt (2016) examined how overconfidence drives speculative bubbles. Using ten experimental markets, they found that overconfident

---

calculated as the difference in abnormal returns between the long and short positions, which serves as an estimate of the strategy's economic profitability. In a perfect market, this return reflects market efficiency, but in reality, constraints like short-selling restrictions can limit its effectiveness (Alexander, 2000, p. 2).

traders create larger bubbles, higher volatility, and excessive trading. Prices in these markets deviate significantly from fundamental values, leading to market crashes. Overconfidence also distorts price forecasting, fueling speculation. However, it declines over time, suggesting that as investors gain more experience, the effects get moderated.

2.3 Post-Earnings Announcement Drift (PEAD) and Limited Investor Attention Bias

The Post-Earnings Announcement Drift (PEAD) is a well-documented anomaly in financial markets, where stock prices gradually adjust to earnings surprises rather than reacting immediately (as predicted by the efficient market hypothesis). This reflects a broader pattern of market underreaction, where stock prices fail to fully incorporate earnings information at the time of release. Wang et al. (2018, p. 2) highlight that this underreaction leads to a sustained price drift, making PEAD one of the most persistent anomalies in asset pricing. The phenomenon has been widely studied for decades (Fink, 2021, p. 1).

Ball and Brown (1968) were among the first to examine the relationship between accounting earnings and stock prices, and they found that stock prices begin to reflect earnings information before its public release, suggesting that markets anticipate earnings news. However, they also observed that stock prices continued to adjust in the direction of the earnings surprise for months after the announcement, a phenomenon now known as the Post-Earnings Announcement Drift (PEAD).

Subsequent research provided further empirical support. Foster, Olsen and Shevlin (1984) showed that firm size and the direction of earnings surprises explain 81% of PEAD. Similarly, Brown and Pope (1996) confirmed that PEAD anomaly is a persistent and significant characteristic of stock returns, correlating with factors like a firm's survival probability and bid-ask spreads.

Bernard and Thomas (1990) challenged prior findings, arguing that stock prices fail to fully incorporate the implications of current earnings for future earnings. They attributed this to investors naively assuming a seasonal random walk, where future earnings are expected to mirror those of the same quarter in the prior year.

However, Ball and Bartov (1996) rejected this view, arguing that investors do not blindly follow a naive seasonal random walk. Instead, they showed that while investors recognize past earnings patterns, they systematically underestimate the strength of serial correlation by about 50%, which contributes to the delayed response in stock prices.

Chan, Jegadeesh and Lakonishok (1996) investigated the relationship between PEAD and momentum strategies[3]. Their study found that abnormal returns following earnings surprises persist for six to twelve months, suggesting that momentum strategies capitalize on delayed price reactions. Using multiple earnings surprise measures, including Standardized Unexpected Earnings (SUE)[4], Cumulative Abnormal Returns (CAR)[5], and analyst forecast changes, they showed that stocks with positive surprises continue to outperform, while those with negative surprises underperform.

Fama[6] acknowledged the robustness of PEAD, stating that "the grand-daddy of under-reaction events is the evidence that stock prices seem to respond to earnings for about a year after they are announced" (Fama, 1998, p. 4 and 25).

The role of investor inattention in explaining PEAD has gained increased attention in behavioural finance research. Hirshleifer, Lim and Teoh (2009) showed that when multiple earnings announcements occur on the same day, the market reaction is weaker, leading to a stronger PEAD effect. Similarly, DellaVigna and Pollet (2009) found that Friday earnings announcements receive weaker immediate reactions, as investors are more distracted, and firms often release bad news on Fridays to take advantage of this inattention. Additionally, earnings announced during trading hours adjust faster than those released after market

[3] Momentum strategies involve trading based on past stock returns or earnings surprises. Price momentum strategies rely on past stock price movements, while earnings momentum strategies are driven by earnings surprises. Both approaches capitalize on the market's tendency to underreact to new information. Specifically, earnings momentum strategies profit from the market's delayed response to short-term earnings announcements, whereas price momentum strategies exploit the gradual adjustment of stock prices to long-term earnings trends (Chan, Jegadeesh and Lakonishok, 1996, pp. 2–3).

[4] Standardized Unexpected Earnings (SUE) is a measure of earnings surprise that quantifies how much a company's reported earnings deviate from market expectations.

[5] Cumulative Abnormal Return (CAR) measures the total abnormal return of a stock around the most recent announcement date.

[6] Eugene Fama is often regarded as "the father of efficient market hypothesis" for his seminal work in rational asset pricing theories in the 1960s. His work later influenced the development of index funds. Fama won the joint Nobel Prize in 2013 with Robert Shiller and Lars Peter Hansen for their work on asset price theories. Fama's research showed that short-term stock price movements are unpredictable, while Shiller, a behavioural economist, showed that stock prices can be forecasted over longer periods. Hansen contributed by developing a statistical method to test these theories, proving that existing models couldn't fully explain Shiller's findings, and his method is now a key tool in economics research (The Nobel Prize, 2013).

close (Pagach and Stephan, 1992, cited in Wang et al., 2018). Wang et al. (2018) tested the PEAD phenomenon in the options market, using pre-announcement option trading as a proxy for investor attention. They found that when investors are highly attentive, PEAD is weaker. In contrast, lower attention results in a more pronounced drift.

PEAD is a global phenomenon (Fink, 2021). Griffin, Kelly, and Nardari (2010) confirm its presence across developed and emerging markets, finding that the magnitude of PEAD is similar across both market types. They argued that investor inattention is the primary driver in developed markets, whereas high transaction costs play a key role in emerging markets.

Similarly, Hung, Li and Wang (2015) found that PEAD is prevalent worldwide, but the degree of influence varies due to market frictions. Their study highlights that investor distraction and arbitrage constraints are the dominant drivers in developed markets, while high transaction costs play a larger role in emerging markets. Additionally, they show that PEAD declines in firms with improved financial reporting, increased analyst forecast accuracy, higher institutional ownership, and lower arbitrage constraints.

2.4 The Behavioural Three-Factor Model

This section will take a closer look at the behavioural three-factor model introduced by Daniel, Hirshleifer and Lin (2020), which serves as the foundation for the empirical analysis in this study.

Daniel, Hirshleifer and Lin (2020), introduced a behavioural three-factor model to explain anomalies in stock returns by incorporating investor psychology into asset pricing. The model complemented the traditional market factor (from the CAPM framework) with two behavioural factors: a long-horizon mispricing factor based on firms' financing decisions (issuances/repurchases or FIN factor) and a short-horizon mispricing factor based on investor underreaction to earnings surprises (Post-Earnings Announcement Drift or PEAD). These factors aim to capture market mispricing driven by investor biases: overconfidence and limited attention, respectively.

Daniel, Hirshleifer and Lin (2020) developed the FIN factor based on the empirical findings of Stein (1996), who suggested that when a firm's stock price is mispriced (either overvalued or undervalued), managers may exploit this market inefficiency by issuing or repurchasing shares without altering the firm's investment levels. If investors were fully rational, they would fully understand and incorporate the reasons behind a firm's decision to issue or repurchase equity into stock prices immediately. As a result, these financing decisions may not have predictive power to determine future stock prices because the market would have already adjusted the prices to reflect this information (Myers and Majluf, 1984). However, in reality, the opposite holds true due to the presence of investor biases.

The FIN factor is designed by considering the return spread between low-financing firms (including repurchasing firms) and high-financing firms. This is based on the empirical observation that, on average, there are persistent and significant negative abnormal returns following issuance activity and positive abnormal returns following repurchases (Daniel, Hirshleifer and Lin, 2020)[7].

The FIN factor is ideal for capturing long-term mispricing because managers make decisions about equity issuances or repurchases in response to persistent mispricing rather than short-term fluctuations. This is because firms face significant frictions in terms of disclosure requirements and legal and underwriting costs when issuing or repurchasing shares, making short-horizon responses to market mispricing impractical. Additionally, there are informational barriers that prevent firms from responding quickly to transient market changes[8]. The fixed costs associated with initiating these corporate actions further limit their use for short-term corrections[9].

The PEAD factor is introduced to capture short-term mispricing that the FIN factor may overlook. It is based on the theory that investors with limited attention underreact to new earnings information, leading to a delayed adjustment in

---

[7] Cited in Daniel, Hirshleifer and Lin (2020): see Loughran and Ritter (1995, 2000), Spiess and Affleck-Graves (1995), Brav, Geczy, and Gompers (2000), and Bradshaw, Richardson, and Sloan (2006) for evidence of post-event underperformance of new issues. For evidence of post-event outperformance of repurchases, see Lakonishok and Vermaelen (1990), Ikenberry, Lakonishok, Vermaelen (1995), and Bradshaw, Richardson, and Sloan (2006). Comprehensive measures of total issuances and repurchases are developed by Daniel and Titman (2006) and Pontiff and Woodgate (2008).

[8] US regulations can cause significant delays in the process of registering new security issues, making it difficult for firms to act quickly on short-term market opportunities. Issuing new shares may also raise concerns among investors, who might suspect that firms are taking advantage of insider knowledge to issue shares when their stock is overvalued (Daniel, Hirshleifer, and Sun, 2020; Myers and Majluf, 1984).

[9] The bigger the overall mispricing, the more profitable it is for a firm to take advantage of it. A mispricing that results in abnormal returns over five years provides a greater opportunity for firms to benefit compared to similar or slightly smaller mispricing that lasts for only one year (Daniel, Hirshleifer and Sun, 2020).

stock prices[10]. Firms with positive earnings surprises tend to earn higher returns, while those with negative surprises see lower returns. Traditional risk factors do not explain this phenomenon but reflect a delayed response to information. The PEAD factor captures this systematic, high-frequency mispricing by forming a portfolio that goes long on firms with positive earnings surprises and short on those with negative surprises. Earnings announcements are an ideal setting to observe short-term underreaction, as they provide consistent, value-relevant updates for every firm each quarter (Daniel, Hirshleifer and Lin, 2020).

Firstly, the authors tested how well their behavioural factor model explained expected stock returns compared to traditional models like the Fama-French and other recent models[11]. Traditional factors include market, size, value, and momentum, while newer factors include investment and profitability. Their model successfully explained many key factors proposed in the literature, showing it captures mispricing better than other models.

Next, they tested how well FIN and PEAD explain the returns of portfolios formed based on 34 well-known stock return anomalies[12]. Since FIN captures long-term mispricing and PEAD captures short-term mispricing, they divided the anomalies into two groups: 12 short-horizon anomalies (such as price momentum and earnings momentum) and 22 long-horizon anomalies (such as value, investment, and long-term profitability). Their model fully explained all 12 short-horizon anomalies at a 5% significance level. In contrast, alternative models, like

---

[10] Daniel, Hirshleifer and Sun (2020); Hirshleifer and Teoh (2003); DellaVigna and Pollet, (2009); Hirshleifer, Lim, and Teoh (2011).

[11] 11Cited in Daniel, Hirshleifer and Lin (2020). The authors compared their behavioural three-factor model with a total of seven well-known factor models, including both traditional and more recently proposed ones. These models include the Fama-French three-factor model (FF3), which incorporates market, size (SMB), and value (HML) factors (Fama and French, 1993); Carhart's four-factor model (Carhart4), which adds a momentum (MOM) factor (Carhart, 1997); Novy-Marx's four-factor model (NM4), which includes market, momentum, profitability (PMU), and a modified value factor (Novy-Marx, 2013); the Fama-French five-factor model (FF5), which extends FF3 by adding profitability (RMW) and investment (CMA) factors (Fama and French, 2015); Hou, Xue, and Zhang's q-factor model (HXZ4), which consists of market, size, investment (IVA), and profitability (ROE) factors (Hou, Xue and Zhang, 2015); and Stambaugh and Yuan's four-factor mispricing model (SY4), which incorporates market, size, and two mispricing factors, one capturing managerial characteristics (MGMT) and another focusing on performance anomalies (PERF) (Stambaugh and Yuan, 2017).

[12] The above comparisons were used to evaluate the model's performance against a broad set of return anomalies, divided into 12 short-horizon and 22 long-horizon anomalies (Daniel, Hirshleifer and Lin, 2020).

the Fama-French five-factor model, failed to explain many of these anomalies. For long-horizon anomalies, their model also performed well.

The authors also hypothesised that FIN and PEAD factors should better explain returns of short-leg portfolios (overpriced stocks) compared to long-leg portfolios (underpriced stocks) because mispricing in overpriced stocks is harder to correct due to short-sale constraints and market frictions such as high transaction costs and borrowing difficulties. These frictions limit an arbitrageur's ability to correct prices, allowing behavioural biases to persist longer in overpriced stocks. Therefore, the authors expected the long-leg portfolios (underpriced) to load positively on FIN and PEAD, and the short-leg portfolios (overpriced) to load negatively. The results supported these hypotheses. For short-horizon anomalies, 11 out of 12 showed larger negative and statistically significant PEAD loadings in the short legs, confirming that PEAD effectively captures short-term mispricing in overpriced stocks. Similarly, in the short leg, 15 out of 22 anomalies showed larger negative and statistically significant FIN loadings. They also saw positive loadings for FIN and PEAD in the long-leg portfolios.

A positive loading on the FIN or PEAD factor indicates that a portfolio is exposed to assets experiencing underpricing and delayed correction, leading to predictable outperformance. Conversely, a negative loading reflects exposure to overpriced stocks where mispricing persists, often resulting in future underperformance.

In summary, Daniel, Hirshleifer and Lin's (2020) behavioural three-factor model effectively addresses short- and long-horizon anomalies in stock returns by incorporating two mispricing factors: FIN for long-term market mispricing through financing decisions and PEAD for short-term mispricing via delayed reactions to earnings surprises. Their model outperforms traditional factor models, such as Fama-French, in explaining return anomalies. The authors also empirically proved that FIN and PEAD are more effective at capturing mispricing in overpriced stocks due to market frictions, confirming that behavioural biases significantly influence stock returns.

2.5 Behavioural Biases During Volatile Market Conditions

This section explores how behavioural biases emerge in extreme market conditions, particularly as sustainability-focused investors may react differently from those holding conventional portfolios. Since this empirical study tests the behaviour of overconfidence and limited attention biases separately during bull and bear markets, this section provides the theoretical foundation.

2.5.1 Post-Earnings Announcement Drift (PEAD) and Limited Attention

Limited investor attention is a key driver of Post-Earnings Announcement Drift (PEAD). In the behavioural three-factor model, a positive loading on the PEAD factor suggests that a portfolio tends to consist of stocks with positive earnings surprises, and that these surprises are followed by continued upward drift in prices; a sign that prices adjust gradually due to investor inattention. In contrast, a negative PEAD loading implies that the portfolio includes stocks with negative earnings surprises that continue to underperform, reflecting a delayed market reaction to poor earnings news. Therefore, positive PEAD coefficients imply the portfolio benefits from attention-driven price corrections, while negative coefficients indicate persistent mispricing due to investor underreaction.

Hou, Peng, and Xiong (2008) show that in bear markets, investors tend to underreact to earnings announcements due to lower attention levels, causing earnings-related information to be incorporated into stock prices slowly over time. This delayed response results in a gradual drift in valuations, reinforcing PEAD effects. Conversely, in bull markets, investor attention is heightened, leading to an overreaction to price momentum, where past winners continue to gain, amplifying stock price movements.

In volatile markets, biases such as the ostrich effect also shape how investors process information. Karlsson, Loewenstein, and Seppi (2009) found that investors avoid checking their portfolios during downturns to shield themselves from the psychological discomfort of negative news. However, in rising markets, investors monitor their portfolios more frequently to derive utility from positive outcomes.

This understanding is crucial when interpreting the effects of limited attention during different market phases, such as bull and bear markets.

2.5.2 Overconfidence in Bull and Bear Markets

In bull markets, increased investor attention fosters overconfidence, affecting how earnings news and market trends are interpreted. As per the behavioural three-factor model, a positive FIN loading indicates exposure to firms that are undervalued (e.g., repurchasing shares) and likely to outperform as prices correct, while a negative FIN loading reflects exposure to overvalued, high-issuance firms that typically underperform due to persistent overpricing.

Gervais and Odean (2001) and Daniel, Hirshleifer and Subrahmanyam (2001) found that overconfidence is more prevalent in bull markets, leading to excessive trading activity. Other empirical findings also confirm that while overconfidence exists in both bull and bear markets, its effects are significantly stronger in bull markets (Chuang and Lee, 2006). As investors become overconfident, they chase past winners, further fueling price momentum and speculative behaviour.

In contrast, during bear markets, lower attention levels reduce overconfident trading behaviour. Instead of chasing trends, investors become more risk-averse and disengaged (Hou, Peng and Xiong, 2008).

The social dimension of investor behaviour further amplifies these effects. Karlsson, Loewenstein, and Seppi (2009) show that during bull markets, frequent portfolio monitoring creates positive feedback loops, where rising prices generate optimism and social buzz, reinforcing overconfidence and speculative trading. In bear markets, however, reduced portfolio monitoring suppresses the spread of negative sentiment, which can prolong downturns as investors remain disengaged.

2.6 Sustainable Finance

Building on the discussion of behavioural biases in investing, this section examines their intersection with sustainable finance. With the growing prominence of Environmental, Social, and Governance (ESG) factors, investment strategies are expanding beyond traditional risk-return considerations. However, as the literature suggests, just as conventional investments are shaped by cognitive biases, sustainability-driven investments are also influenced by behavioural factors. This section introduces the theoretical background in sustainable finance, analyzes the EU-US ESG gap, presents evidence of biases in sustainable finance, and explores how behavioural biases impact sustainability fund returns during extreme market events.

Sustainable Finance—Theoretical Background

Sustainable finance involves incorporating environmental, social, and governance (ESG) factors into investment decision-making within the financial sector. This approach promotes long-term investments that support sustainable economic activities and projects (European Union, n.d.).

Stakeholder theory and legitimacy theory are key theoretical frameworks in sustainability discussions. Stakeholder theory (Freeman, 1984) argues that businesses should consider the interests of all stakeholders (employees, customers, communities, and shareholders) rather than focusing solely on profit. As per Hörisch, Freeman and Schaltegger (2014), engaging with stakeholders enhances sustainability and long-term success. Legitimacy theory suggests that businesses seek societal approval by aligning their actions with public expectations (Suchman, 1995). Deegan (2020) found that companies tend to increase social and environmental disclosures in response to media scrutiny, suggesting that firms strategically communicate sustainability efforts to maintain public trust and legitimacy.

One of the most rapidly evolving areas in sustainable finance is Sustainable and Responsible Investment (SRI) funds. These funds commonly rely on ESG ratings to shape their investment strategies. The SRI industry is experiencing significant growth and is expected to reach $35 trillion by 2025 (Ciciretti, Dalò and Ferri, 2023).

2.7 EU—US ESG Gap: Region Bias

There is a distinct difference in ESG ratings between the EU and the US firms. According to LaBella et al. (2019, p. 1), ESG ratings typically exhibit a size and region bias, favouring large-cap and Europe-based companies. Other studies have also found evidence of size bias (Drempetic, Klein, and Zwergel, 2020; Giese et al., 2019) and the EU's regional bias (Doyle, 2018). As per Ciciretti, Dalò and Ferri (2023), EU-listed companies outperform US firms by 14% on average ESG score, mainly in the Environmental (+22.5%) and Social (+16%) dimensions, with negligible differences in Governance (+0.4%). This advantage arises from stricter EU non-financial disclosure regulations, such as Directive 2014/95/EU, along with subsequent regulations and guidelines, which have led to significant improvements in sustainability reporting, particularly for larger companies and corporate groups. Before its enforcement, 62.29% of EU firms reported ESG data under GRI standards, compared to only 44.86% of US firms (Ciciretti, Dalò and Ferri, 2023).

In contrast, ESG reporting in the US remains voluntary unless financially material, limiting transparency (US SEC, 2010, cited in Ciciretti, Dalò and Ferri, 2023). However, mandatory EU reporting may reduce its credibility as a true signal of sustainability commitment. In the US, voluntary disclosures act as a stronger green commitment indicator (D'Apice, Ferri and Lipari, 2020; Ciciretti, Dalò and Ferri, 2023).

The global ESG reporting landscape is evolving. The introduction of IFRS S1(IFRS Sustainability Reporting Disclosure Standard) and S2 (IFRS Climate-Related Disclosure Standard) marks a significant step toward the global standardization of sustainability reporting. Effective January 1, 2024, these standards integrate financial and sustainability reporting into a company's corporate reporting for the first time (Pratama et al., 2024). EY (2024) notes that mandatory adoption will depend on each jurisdiction's endorsement or regulatory processes. However, the global implementation of IFRS sustainability standards could harmonize sustainability reporting practices, enhance transparency and comparability, and help bridge regional ESG disclosure gaps, including those between the EU and the US.

2.8 Evidence of Biases in Sustainable Finance

ESG investments are driven by various motivations. Beal, Goyen and Phillips (2005) identified three primary motivations: financial returns, social transformation, and non-wealth (psychic) returns. While financial returns remain an essential requirement for investment, investors may trade off financial gains for ethical satisfaction. Psychic returns, such as an increase in happiness due to ethical investing, further complicate investment choices and introduce biases into decision-making.

Nilsson (2009) expanded on this by classifying ESG investors into three groups: (1) financially motivated investors, (2) those with mixed objectives, and (3) altruistically motivated investors. Notably, not all ESG investors prioritize social responsibility over profit maximization. Some ESG investors select sustainable investments solely for financial gains, while others deliberately accept lower returns to align with their ethical values. This suggests that behavioural finance plays a role in distinguishing ESG investors based on their motivations.

One key bias affecting ESG investing is overconfidence. Investors who strongly believe in their ability to assess ESG factors may assign greater importance to their own perspectives than to external viewpoints (Sultana et al., 2018). Research on Pakistani stock market investors found that overconfident investors emphasize ESG factors in their decision-making, sometimes to the extent of disregarding broader market signals (Rooh et al., 2023). This aligns with previous findings that overconfident investors tend to hold on to ESG investments despite market fluctuations (Daugaard, 2019).

Herd behaviour is another psychological bias prevalent in ESG investing. Investors often follow the market trend, assuming that if most investors are pursuing ESG investments, these must be fundamentally sound (Rubbaniy et al., 2021). This behaviour is observed even in emerging markets such as Pakistan, where investors continue to exhibit herd behaviour despite being aware of ESG-oriented equities (Rooh et al., 2023). Additionally, the presence of large SRI fund families can amplify this behaviour, leading to greater fund flow volatility (Renneboog et al., 2011). Gavrilakis and Floros (2024) found that European ESG leaders' portfolio exhibits herding behaviour, which results in reduced diversification benefits and increased risk exposure, making it more difficult to hedge.

Loss aversion plays a crucial role in ESG investment decisions. Investors tend to allocate capital to environmentally responsible firms due to the perception that such firms are financially stable and less likely to incur losses (Dash and Kajiji, 2020). Rooh et al. (2023) found that Pakistani investors exhibiting loss aversion prefer ESG-oriented companies, as they associate these firms with lower financial risk. This finding aligns with previous research indicating that investors seek to mitigate risk by prioritizing ESG-conscious investments (Marti-Ballester, 2015).

Behavioural biases in ESG investing are particularly pronounced in emerging markets, where investor awareness and regulatory frameworks are still developing. Deka et al. (2023) investigated Indian retail investors and found that risk perception significantly influences equity investment decisions. Importantly, ESG consciousness moderates the impact of biases on risk perception, suggesting that investors with a high ESG awareness are less likely to be swayed by psychological biases. Similar patterns are observed in Pakistani investors, where herd behaviour and overconfidence impact ESG investment choices (Rooh et al., 2023).

Recent studies suggest that European high-ESG firms are not exposed to overconfidence and limited attention biases; however, low-ESG firms are exposed to overconfidence bias (Badía, Goicoechea, and Ugarte 2024).

2.9 Behavioural Biases and ESG Fund Performance in Extreme Markets

SRI performance varies across market conditions, which can be explained through behavioural finance, particularly Prospect Theory. Investors are more sensitive to losses than gains (Kahneman and Tversky, 1979), influencing investment decisions during crises.

Nofsinger and Varma (2012) analyzed SRI mutual funds from 2000 to 2011, finding that conventional funds outperformed SRI funds by 0.67% to 0.95% annually in stable periods. However, during crises, SRI funds outperformed conventional funds by 1.61% to 1.70%, suggesting they provide downside protection. ESG-focused funds, particularly those using positive screening techniques, performed best, while exclusionary or faith-based funds showed weaker results. The researchers concluded that the asymmetric returns of SRI funds, along with investor behaviour explained by Prospect Theory, provide a plausible explanation for their growing popularity (Nofsinger and Varma, 2012).

3 Methodology and Data

In this chapter, the theoretical background of the study's methodology, key model variables, modifications introduced to the three-factor model to examine the intersection between sustainable investments and behavioural biases, and data sources used in this study will be discussed.

3.1 Theoretical Background

This study is based on the behavioural three-factor model introduced by Daniel, Hirshleifer and Sun (2020) and its application to European sustainable firms by Badía, Goicoechea and Ugarte (2024). The behavioural three-factor model expands traditional asset pricing frameworks by incorporating two mispricing factors driven by investor psychology, alongside the conventional market factor. These mispricing factors account for long-term mispricing due to overconfidence bias (FIN factor) and short-term underreaction resulting from limited attention bias (PEAD factor).

While Badía, Goicoechea, and Ugarte (2024) analyzed multiple ESG portfolios based on various ESG score cut-off thresholds (Top and Bottom 10%, 20%, 30%) and ran separate regressions for each of the six portfolios, this study takes a slightly different approach by adopting a binary classification, using a dummy variable to distinguish between high-ESG (Top 10%) and low-ESG (Bottom 10%) portfolio returns. The use of a dummy variable, along with interaction terms, offers a more focused and efficient way to analyze whether behavioural biases affect ESG leaders and laggards differently within a single regression model.

R.M. V. Bandaranayake, *The Differential Impact of Investor Behavioural Biases on US Sustainable and Non-Sustainable Firms*, BestMasters,
https://doi.org/10.1007/978-3-658-50668-1_3

3.2 Data

ESG Scores

This study examines the susceptibility of publicly listed firms in the United States to behavioural biases, differentiating between sustainable and non-sustainable firms. Sustainability is assessed using ESG scores provided by the Thomson Reuters Refinitiv ESG scoring framework. Refinitiv calculates ESG scores using a data-driven methodology that evaluates a company's ESG performance across ten key themes, such as emissions, human rights, and shareholder governance. The ESG score is based on 178 selected measures from over 400 ESG data points sourced from publicly available company reports, sustainability disclosures, and third-party data providers. The ESG pillar scores (Environmental, Social, and Governance) are aggregated using a percentile ranking methodology and benchmarked against industry peers (for E and S scores) and country peers (for G scores) (Thomson Reuters, 2018, p. 3–13).

This study covers a broad US dataset, covering nearly 1,400 publicly listed firms across all industries except financials with an ESG scoring. The exclusion of financial firms from the sample is due to their unique regulatory environment and financial structures, which make their financing decisions primarily driven by regulatory requirements rather than market mispricing. The sample spans nearly two decades, from June 2005 to June 2023, allowing the identification of behavioural biases over a long period. This extended period provides a more comprehensive analysis of market behaviour, including bull and bear market phases. Like Badía, Goicoechea and Ugarte (2024), this study also includes active and inactive firms in the entire Refinitiv universe to mitigate survivorship bias and ensure more representative and unbiased analysis.

Table 3.1 shows the evolution of ESG scores every three years. ESG scores, as provided by Refinitiv, range from 0 to 100, where higher scores represent stronger performance in environmental, social, and governance metrics. This 0–100 scale enables comparison across firms and time.

Unsurprisingly, higher percentile rankings correlate with higher average ESG scores. The consistent growth between percentiles over time shows the reliability of the dataset. Consistent with Badía, Cortez, and Ferruz (2020), the growing number of rated firms indicates increased market demand for ESG data. The overall improvement in ESG scores, coupled with the increasing number of rated firms over time, indicates that companies are paying attention to ESG factors and achieving better ratings.

Table 3.1 Evolution of ESG Scores

	P10	P20	P30	P70	P80	P90	Median	Mean	S.D.	No of firms
2005	14.19	17.92	20.51	33.90	40.42	47.89	26.96	29.40	13.64	201
2008	15.37	21.89	26.94	51.17	57.61	67.16	38.33	39.96	19.15	257
2011	18.06	24.12	29.65	54.03	63.63	74.11	39.79	43.12	20.52	376
2014	17.33	24.53	31.60	56.74	66.78	74.70	42.87	44.85	20.70	401
2017	14.65	19.77	24.39	46.50	57.38	68.81	33.86	38.04	20.04	878
2020	16.15	21.82	27.66	51.50	61.06	71.28	38.24	41.18	20.56	1169
2023	14.74	23.32	30.05	57.42	64.60	72.51	43.13	43.85	21.11	1411

1 This table provides a summary of ESG score percentiles and descriptive statistics for the US firms included in the sample. All US publicly traded companies (except financial firms) with an ESG score are included. The sample period is from June 2005 to June 2023

3.3 Portfolio Formation

Similar to the approach taken by Badía, Goicoechea and Ugarte (2024), the author constructed two value-weighted portfolios, a high-ESG portfolio and a low-ESG portfolio, based on their ESG scores, respectively. The companies were sorted each year based on the ESG scores of the preceding year, and the Top 10% and the Bottom 10% of the sample universe in each year were chosen. In this exercise, firms which had a closing share price of USD 1 or less were excluded to minimize microstructure-induced biases. Portfolios were rebalanced at the end of June in each calendar year based on market capitalization and ESG scores. Rebalancing portfolios at the end of June is a commonly established academic practice to avoid look-ahead bias. Thereby, anomaly portfolios are typically formed in June to ensure that financial statement information would be publicly available at the time of portfolio formation (Bowles et al., 2024, p. 4). Monthly discrete total returns for the constituent stocks in the portfolios were obtained from Refinitiv. Portfolio returns were then computed as the weighted sum of these returns, with weights reflecting the portfolio allocation for each stock.

Table 3.2 shows a clear distinction in ESG scores between high-ESG (top 10%) and low-ESG (bottom 10%) firms from 2005 to 2023. High-ESG firms consistently maintain much higher scores, with mean values rising from 59.36 in 2005 to 78.53 in 2023. In contrast, low-ESG firms' scores remain significantly low, with the mean increasing from 8.89 in 2005 to 12.52 in 2023.

Table 3.2 Portfolio-wise ESG Scores

	Mean		Median		Max		Min	
	Top 10%	Bottom 10%	Top 10%	Bottom 10%	Top 10%	Bottom 10%	Top 10%	Bottom 10%
2005	59.36	8.89	55.26	8.76	85.80	12.36	51.39	3.96
2008	73.14	10.87	71.42	12.33	88.73	15.45	63.32	2.02
2011	79.54	12.36	78.19	14.08	94.93	16.64	72.89	2.37
2014	79.40	13.05	77.76	14.36	91.31	18.80	72.91	1.35
2017	77.40	11.90	77.26	12.55	91.06	16.63	69.61	0.85
2020	77.39	11.51	76.34	12.27	93.06	15.29	69.74	0.62
2023	78.53	12.52	77.81	13.20	92.80	16.93	71.93	3.07

This table shows the mean, median, maximum, and minimum ESG scores for the top 10% (ESG leaders) and bottom 10%

3.4 Behavioural Biases (FIN and PEAD)

3.4.1 The FIN Factor

The FIN factor captures long-term mispricing and looks at the return spread between recent issuers and repurchases. Daniel, Hirshleifer and Sun (2020) constructed the FIN factor by combining the 1-year net-share-issuance (NSI) metric introduced by Pontiff and Woodgate (2008) with the 5-year composite-share-issuance (CSI) measure from Daniel and Titman (2006). The CSI metric calculates a firm's 5-year market equity growth minus its 5-year equity return, in logarithms. Issuance activities such as equity offerings, employee stock option schemes and equity-financed acquisitions increase the issuance measure, whereas activities like share buybacks, cash dividend payments and other cash distributions reduce it. Corporate actions such as stock splits and stock dividends do not affect the market capitalization or returns and, therefore, have no impact on the composite issuance measure. Pontiff and Woodgate's NSI metric is similar to CSI, but is based on a 1-year horizon and excludes cash dividends. The CSI and NSI metrics are as follows.

$$\mathrm{CSI_t} = \log\left(\mathrm{ME_t}/\mathrm{ME_{t-5}}\right) - \mathrm{r}\,(\mathrm{t}-5,\ \mathrm{t}) \tag{3.1}$$

For the CSI calculation in June of year *t*, ME_t represents the market equity at the end of June in year t, ME_{t-5} denotes the market equity at the end of June in year

$t-5$ and $r(t-5,t)$ refers to the cumulative log return of the stock from the end of June in year $t-5$ to the end of June in year t.

Pontiff and Woodgate's NSI measure is the same as the CSI, except that it uses a 1-year time frame and does not include cash dividends.

$$\mathrm{NSI}_{t-1} = \log\left(\text{split-adjusted shares outstanding} / \text{split-adjusted shares outstanding}_{t-1}\right) \quad (3.2)$$

Once CSI and NSI are calculated, the firms are assigned to three financing groups (low "L", middle "M" or high "H") based on an index of NSI and CSI rankings. After that, in the spirit of Fama French empirical asset pricing, 2 × 3 portfolios are formed based on the size and financing groups (SL, SM, SH, BL, BM and BH). These six portfolios will be rebalanced at the end of each June. The FIN factor return for each month is computed as the difference between the average return of the low financing portfolios (SL and BL) and the average return of the high financing portfolios (SH and BH).

$$\mathrm{FIN} = (\mathrm{r_{SL}} + \mathrm{r_{BL}})/2 - (\mathrm{r_{SH}} + \mathrm{r_{BH}})/2 \quad (3.3)$$

The author used the monthly FIN factor dataset published by Lin Sun, co-author of Daniel, Hirshleifer and Sun (2020), for this study. The FIN factor is constructed using all common stocks listed on the NYSE, AMEX, and NASDAQ, identified by CRSP common share codes 10 or 11, while excluding financial firms and firms with negative book equity. This data sample is largely identical to the Refinitiv dataset used to obtain ESG scores and construct the two ESG portfolios.

3.4.2 The PEAD Factor

The PEAD factor reflects short-term mispricing due to investors' limited attention bias. The negative/ positive earnings surprises are first calculated, and then 2 × 3 sort portfolios are created following the empirical standard set by Fama and French (1992). Earnings surprise is calculated based on Cumulative Abnormal Returns (CAR) around the most recent quarterly announcement date, as suggested by Chan, Jegadeesh, and Lakonishok (1996, cited in Daniel, Hirshleifer, and Sun, 2020).

$$CAR_i = \sum_{d=-2}^{d=1} (R_{i,d} - R_{m,d}) \quad (3.4)$$

In the formula, $R_{i,d}$ represents the return of stock i on day d, while $R_{m,d}$ shows the market return on day d relative to the earnings announcement.

To construct the PEAD factor portfolio for month t, daily returns are required for at least two of the four trading days around earnings announcements, and the earnings date must be at least two trading days before month-end. Firms with no earnings announcement in the past six months are excluded. Eligible stocks (NYSE, AMEX, NASDAQ, excluding financials) are sorted into size groups (small "S" or big "B") based on market equity relative to the NYSE median and into earnings surprise groups (low "L," middle "M," or high "H") using CAR_i breakpoints (20% and 80%). Six value-weighted portfolios are created, and the PEAD factor return is the average return of high-low surprise portfolios.

$$\text{PEAD} = (\text{r}_{\text{SH}} + \text{r}_{\text{BH}})/2 - (\text{r}_{\text{SL}} + \text{r}_{\text{BL}})/2 \tag{3.5}$$

The author used the monthly PEAD factor dataset published by Lin Sun, co-author of Daniel, Hirshleifer and Sun (2020), for this study.

The data for the market factor in the model (as reflected by Excess Market Return) was obtained from Kenneth French online data library. The excess return on the market is calculated considering the value-weight return of all CRSP firms incorporated in the US and listed on the NYSE, AMEX, or NASDAQ that have a CRSP share code of 10 or 11 minus the one-month Treasury bill rate.

3.5 The Behavioural Three-Factor Model

Daniel, Hirshleifer and Sun's (2020) behavioural three-factor model is as follows:

$$r_{p,t} = \alpha_p + \beta_1 Mkt_t + \beta_2 FIN_t + \beta_3 PEAD_t + \epsilon_{p,t} \tag{3.6}$$

In this model, r_{pt} represents the excess return of portfolio p in month t, calculated relative to the US Treasury yield. Mkt_t indicates the excess return of the value-weighted market portfolio. The model includes the financing factor (FIN) and the Post-Earnings announcement drift (PEAD) as independent variables, with factors constructed from all sampled firms. Here, α_p reflects the intercept, while β_1, β_2 and β_3 measure the portfolio's sensitivity to the independent variables. Lastly, ε_{pt} captures the zero-mean residuals, accounting for unexplained return variations.

The FIN factor specifically addresses long-term mispricing, based on the notion that company managers, aware of their firm's mispricing, may try to exploit it by issuing or repurchasing shares. In contrast, the PEAD factor shows short-term mispricing, where companies that experience positive earnings surprises tend to generate higher returns than those with negative surprises.

3.6 The Modified Model with a Dummy Variable

The author's modified model is based on the behavioural three-factor model introduced by Daniel, Hirshleifer and Sun (2020) and replicates it to distinguish the difference in investor behavioural biases towards high-ESG and low-ESG firms. The high-ESG and low-ESG portfolios are constructed similarly to the approach of Badía, Goicoechea and Ugarte (2024) using Refinitiv ESG scores. Badía, Goicoechea and Ugarte (2024) used six portfolios in varying ESG degrees (Top and Bottom 10%, 20% and 30%) based on different cut-off levels for ESG scores and regressed them against Daniel, Hirshleifer and Sun (2020) three-factor model separately. In this study, instead of six portfolios, only two portfolios are considered (Top 10% and Bottom 10% based on ESG scores, thereby distinguishing between ESG leaders and laggards, and the returns of the portfolios will be regressed against the three-factor model, with a newly introduced dummy variable, as an independent variable. A dummy variable is a constructed variable used in regression analysis to represent a categorical attribute with two or more distinct levels (Skrivanek, 2009).

By introducing a single regression with an interaction term, our model captures nuanced differences in how high- and low-ESG firms are affected by behavioural biases and their influence on portfolio returns. This approach offers a clearer lens into the role of ESG in shaping investor decisions, while maintaining the rigour of earlier methods. The modified three-factor model is:

$$\begin{aligned} r_{p,t} =& \alpha_p + \beta_1 (R_{Mkt} - R_f) + \beta_2 FIN_t + \beta_3 PEAD_t + \beta_4 D \\ &+ \beta_5 D \cdot (R_{Mkt} - R_f) + \beta_6 D \cdot FIN_t + \beta_7 D \cdot PEAD_t + \epsilon_p \end{aligned} \tag{3.7}$$

In the modified model, r_{pt} represents the excess return of portfolio p (high-ESG and low-ESG) in month t, calculated relative to the 1-month US Treasury yield. Mkt_t denotes the excess return of the value-weighted market portfolio, while FIN_t and $PEAD_t$ capture the financing factor and post-earnings announcement drift, respectively. The dummy variable D is introduced to distinguish between high-ESG and low-ESG portfolios, which takes a value of 1 for high-ESG and 0 for low-ESG portfolios. Interaction terms involving D allow for analysing differences in sensitivities to the independent variables across ESG classifications. In this model, α_p reflects the intercept, while β_1, β_2, β_3, β_4, β_5, β_6, and β_7 measure sensitivities to the respective variables and their interactions. Lastly, ε_{pt} captures the zero-mean residuals, accounting for unexplained return variations.

4 Results and Discussion

In this chapter, the main findings of this study will be discussed, supported by theoretical reasoning.

4.1 Descriptive Statistics

The descriptive statistics of the key variables used in the factor model are presented in Table 4.1. The dependent variable includes the monthly excess returns of high-ESG and low-ESG portfolios. The main independent variables include the monthly market excess return and the two behavioural factors, PEAD and FIN. The table reports the mean, median, standard deviation, minimum and maximum values, skewness and excess kurtosis and 5% and 95% percentiles of each variable.

Market excess return (market return over risk-free returns) accounts for the highest average return premium (0.794), solidifying its role as the primary systematic risk factor in asset pricing models. However, the high standard deviation (4.538) indicates substantial return variation, reflecting market-wide volatility.

R.M. V. Bandaranayake, *The Differential Impact of Investor Behavioural Biases on US Sustainable and Non-Sustainable Firms*, BestMasters,
https://doi.org/10.1007/978-3-658-50668-1_4

The average return premiums of the two behavioural factors are notably low compared to the average market return (systematic risk). The FIN factor has a higher average premium (0.294) compared to PEAD (0.162), but this comes with greater return dispersion, as indicated by the former's high standard deviation.

Table 4.2 shows the correlation between the main variables. An important observation is that the level of correlation between the FIN and PEAD factors is low at −0.040 for low-ESG firms. Similarly, for high-ESG firms, the correlation between interacting terms for PEAD and FIN shows a low negative correlation (−0.036). This indicates that the two behavioural factors capture different sources of mispricing.

Both behavioural factors show low correlations with the Market Excess Return factor. This suggests that these behavioural mispricing are less sensitive to overall market movements and are mainly driven by company-specific actions (idiosyncratic risks).

Table 4.1 Descriptive Statistics of the Variables in the Factor Model

	Mean	Median	S.D.	Min	Max	Skewness	Ex. Kurtosis	5% Perc.	95% Perc.
Portfolio_ Excess Return (High-ESG & Low-ESG)	0.731	1.132	5.314	−24.108	27.243	−0.383	4.530	−7.922	7.841
Market_ Excess Return	0.794	1.230	4.538	−17.230	13.650	−0.559	1.285	−8.120	7.720
PEAD	0.162	0.092	2.139	−9.028	7.710	−0.130	1.837	−3.049	3.292
FIN	0.294	−0.168	3.260	−6.843	10.689	0.774	0.875	−4.824	6.312

This table shows the descriptive statistics for the dependent variable (high- and low-ESG portfolio excess returns) and independent variables from the three-factor model from Daniel, Hirshleifer and Lin (2020). The full period analyzed is from June 2005 to June 2023

Table 4.2 Correlations between the Variables in the Factor Model

	Mkt Excess Retun	PEAD	FIN	ESG_ Dummy	ESG_ Dummy_ Market ExcessReturn	ESG_ Dummy PEAD	ESG_ Dummy FIN
Mkt_ Excess Retun	1.000	−0.290	−0.291	0.000	0.702	−0.205	−0.206
PEAD		1.000	−0.040	0.000	−0.203	0.706	−0.028
FIN			1.000	0.000	−0.204	−0.028	0.706
ESG_ Dummy				1.000	0.123	0.054	0.064
ESG_ Dummy * Mkt_ Excess Retun					1.000	−0.281	−0.281
ESG_ Dummy * PEAD						1.000	−0.036
ESG_ Dummy * FIN							1.000

This table shows pairwise correlation for the three-factor model from Daniel, Hirshleifer and Lin (2020). The ESG Dummy variable takes the value of 1 for high-ESG and 0 for low-ESG portfolio returns. The full period analyzed is from June 2005 to June 2023

4.2 Discussion

The regression results presented in Table 4.3 provide a comprehensive analysis of how behavioural biases affect the returns of high-ESG (sustainable) and low-ESG (non-sustainable) portfolios in the US stock market.

Table 4.3 Regression Estimates of the Factor Model

	coefficient	std. error	t-ratio	p-value	
Constant (α)	−0.036	0.174	−0.207	0.836	
ESG_Dummy	0.014	0.247	0.058	0.954	
Market_Excess Return	1.075	0.041	26.312	1.83e-91	***
PEAD	−0.268	0.083	−3.227	0.001	***
FIN	−0.243	0.054	−4.455	1.07e-05	***
ESG_Dummy * Market_Excess Return	−0.162	0.058	−2.802	0.005	***
ESG_Dummy * PEAD	0.378	0.117	3.219	0.001	***
ESG_Dummy * FIN	0.375	0.077	4.869	1.58e-06	***
R-squared	0.7854				
Adjusted R-squared	0.7819				

This table shows the regression estimates of the three-factor model from Daniel, Hirshleifer and Lin (2020) for high-ESG (Top 10%) and low-ESG (Bottom 10%) portfolios. The ESG Dummy variable takes the value of 1 for high-ESG and 0 for low-ESG portfolio returns. Asterisks represent statistically significant coefficients at the 0.1% (***), 1% (**) and 5% (*) significance levels. The full period analyzed is from June 2005 to June 2023

The dummy variable in the regression takes a value of 1 for the high-ESG portfolio and 0 for the low-ESG portfolio, allowing for a separate interpretation of the factor loadings for each group. The model includes the market excess return (Mkt_Excess Return), Post-Earnings Announcement Drift (PEAD), and Financing (FIN) factor, along with interaction terms that capture the differential impact of the behavioural biases on high-ESG portfolios. The adjusted R-squared of 78.19% suggests that the model provides a strong fit, explaining a significant share of variations in portfolio returns.

The regression results show two key insights. The first is that, in the US, both high-ESG and low-ESG firms are exposed to limited attention and overconfidence biases, as indicated by high statistical significance for PEAD and FIN factors (including the interacting terms). This finding differs from the EU experience, where high-ESG firms are not exposed to overconfidence and limited attention biases (Badía, Goicoechea and Ugarte, 2024). This will be discussed in detail in the next section.

The second insight is the difference in factor loadings (beta coefficients) for the two behavioural factors. The regression results show that the low-ESG portfolio exhibits negative factor loadings for both PEAD and FIN, whereas the high-ESG portfolio shows the opposite pattern. This finding is novel.

To better understand this phenomenon, it is important to interpret what positive or negative loadings on the FIN and PEAD factors signify for high-ESG and low-ESG portfolios.

The FIN (Financing) factor is a proxy for long-term mispricing, linked to overconfidence bias. **A positive FIN loading suggests** that **a portfolio behaves similarly to firms that are undervalued and repurchasing shares (i.e., low issuers).** This is typically associated with higher future returns as prices gradually correct. Therefore, a positive FIN coefficient indicates that the portfolio tends to include firms experiencing long-term underpricing, and investors eventually realise this undervaluation. In contrast, a **negative FIN loading implies that the portfolio resembles high-issuance firms, those issuing equity, often at inflated prices due to overconfident market sentiment.** Such firms are usually overvalued and tend to underperform over time. Therefore, a negative FIN coefficient signals exposure to long-term overpricing driven by investor overconfidence, suggesting persistent mispricing and poor future returns.

The PEAD (Post-Earnings Announcement Drift) factor captures short-term mispricing stemming from limited investor attention. **A positive PEAD loading** suggests that the portfolio tends to hold **firms with positive earnings surprises whose prices adjust gradually, indicating an ability to capture upward price drifts due to investor underreaction**. This reflects more efficient price correction, particularly in portfolios where market attention eventually aligns with fundamentals. Conversely, **a negative PEAD loading implies exposure to stocks with negative earnings surprises and slow price adjustments, often due to ignored or misinterpreted earnings signals.** A negative PEAD coefficient points to persistent mispricing due to limited attention, where investors fail to fully digest earnings news, resulting in underperformance.

As per the regression results in this study, the negative and statistically significant PEAD coefficient (−0.268) suggests that low-ESG firms exhibit a price reaction opposite to the typical post-earnings drift effect. Instead of continuing in the direction of an earnings surprise, stock prices of low-ESG firms tend to move against expectations, with positive surprises followed by weaker returns and negative surprises followed by stronger returns. Similarly, the negative and highly significant FIN coefficient (−0.243) indicates that low-ESG firms engaging in low issuance activities (share repurchases) tend to underperform over the long run[1], indicating that their mispricing is more persistent and takes longer to correct.

In contrast, the positive and statistically significant interaction terms for high-ESG portfolios: PEAD (0.378) and FIN (0.375), indicate that high-ESG firms exhibit a more efficient anomaly correction process in response to firms' earnings surprises or financing decisions.

While there is no conclusive evidence in the literature specifically addressing the differences in PEAD and FIN factor loadings between high- and low-ESG portfolios, empirical research by Daniel, Hirshleifer and Sun (2020) provides a framework to interpret these findings. Their study showed that certain portfolios tend to exhibit negative PEAD and FIN loadings due to high arbitrage frictions, which can delay price corrections. Specifically, short-leg portfolios (overpriced/overvalued stocks) remain mispriced for longer due to short-sale constraints, whereas long-leg portfolios (underpriced/undervalued stocks) generally have positive factor loadings. As these behavioural anomalies correct over time (PEAD in the short run and FIN in the long run), short-leg portfolios tend to underperform, while long-leg portfolios benefit from price adjustments.

Applying this framework to ESG portfolios, the negative factor loadings seen in low-ESG portfolios suggest that they resemble characteristics similar to short-leg portfolios, with high arbitrage frictions that slow down mispricing corrections. Several factors may contribute to this inefficiency, such as low institutional participation, reduced information transparency, low disclosure levels and limited access to capital. These structural inefficiencies among ESG laggards may make it more difficult for arbitrageurs to exploit mispricing, resulting in persistent pricing anomalies and delayed price corrections relative to high-ESG firms. The statistical significance of these negative factor loadings further supports the view that market frictions play a critical role in correcting the mispricing associated with low-ESG firms.

On the other hand, the positive and statistically significant interaction terms for the high-ESG portfolio suggest that high-ESG firms behave more like long-leg portfolios, where price adjustments occur more efficiently. The presence of stronger institutional participation, higher transparency, and increased disclosure levels in high-ESG firms is likely to result in a relatively efficient correction of mispricing over time. These findings open an interesting avenue for future research, particularly in understanding the role of ESG characteristics in

---

[1] Empirical evidence shows that, on average, share repurchases lead to positive abnormal returns, while share issuances are followed by persistent and strong negative abnormal returns (Daniel, Hirshleifer and Sun, 2020).

influencing market frictions, price discovery and correction of anomalies over time.

The Market Excess Return coefficient for low-ESG firms is high (1.075) and statistically significant, indicating that market movements strongly influence the returns of low-ESG firms. However, the interaction term (ESG Dummy * Market_ Excess Return) has a highly significant negative coefficient (−0.162), suggesting that high-ESG portfolios are less sensitive to overall market fluctuations. This reduced sensitivity implies that high-ESG portfolios offer better downside protection during periods of market volatility. Therefore, investing in high-ESG firms may serve as an effective tool for risk mitigation and portfolio diversification, helping to reduce overall portfolio risk.

In terms of alpha, the regression results show that high-ESG portfolios have slightly higher returns than low-ESG portfolios, as reflected in the alpha term (−0.036 for low-ESG and −0.022 for high-ESG). However, this difference (β_4 = 0.014, p-value = 0.954 for the ESG_Dummy variable) is statistically insignificant, indicating no meaningful excess return advantage for the high-ESG portfolio. The alpha approaches zero when portfolio returns are fully explained by the included factors (Daniel, Hirshleifer and Sun, 2020, p. 18), and this result suggests that market and behavioural factors, rather than ESG characteristics, drive portfolio performance. Thus, while the high-ESG portfolio exhibits a marginally high return premium, it cannot be confidently attributed to ESG factors alone.

In summary, the regression results show that both high- and low-ESG firms in the US are subject to overconfidence and limited attention biases. However, the similarities end there. While high-ESG portfolios are better positioned to benefit from the correction of behavioural mispricing (as indicated by the statistically significant and positive factor loading), low-ESG portfolios are more prone to persistent mispricing (as indicated by the statistically significant negative factor loading), possibly due to higher arbitrage frictions. As a result, high-ESG portfolios are expected to have an incrementally positive impact on returns when these anomalies are corrected in the future.

4.3 Comparison of Regression Estimates of the Factor Model—EU vs. US

Table 4.4 shows the regression estimates of the EU study and Table 4.5 compares the regression estimates of the behavioural three-factor model between the US and the EU. The EU estimates are based on the empirical findings of Badía, Goicoechea and Ugarte (2024).

The first key difference between the two regions is that, in the EU, low-ESG firms are prone to biases, and high-ESG firms are insulated from the said two biases. This is evidenced by the lack of statistical significance for PEAD and FIN in the Top 10% ESG portfolio in the EU. Their findings remained consistent for high-ESG portfolios in the EU across different cut-off levels (Top 10%, 20%, 30%) (refer to Table 4.4). As a result, Badía, Goicoechea, and Ugarte (2024) concluded that the stock prices of European high-ESG firms are more aligned with the efficient market hypothesis. **In contrast, in the US, the two behavioural biases are present and statistically significant for both ESG leaders and laggards.**

Table 4.4 Regression Estimates of the Factor Model (EU Study)

	α		β_{Mkt}		β_{FIN}		β_{PEAD}	R^2 Adj.
T10	0.0002		1.0343	***	0.0479		-0.0141	0.8944
	(0.1558)		(29.8054)		(0.6624)		(-0.2242)	
B10	0.0035		1.0417	***	-0.4831	***	-0.1652	0.7307
	(1.5853)		(16.2147)		(-4.8154)		(-1.1255)	
L-S10	-0.0033		-0.0074		0.5310	***	0.1511	0.0620
	(-1.2935)		(-0.0854)		(3.9535)		(0.8308)	
T20	0.0003		1.0360	***	0.0406		-0.0043	0.9248
	(0.3478)		(33.5415)		(0.6894)		(-0.0890)	
B20	0.0043	*	0.9965	***	-0.5127	***	-0.1145	0.8327
	(2.5622)		(21.7919)		(-5.8553)		(-1.1667)	
L-S20	-0.0040	*	0.0394		0.5533	***	0.1102	0.1286
	(-2.0762)		(0.6239)		(5.6756)		(0.8457)	
T30	0.0003		1.0413	***	0.0022		-0.0131	0.9398
	(0.3320)		(40.7351)		(0.0414)		(-0.3547)	
B30	0.0032	*	1.0071	***	-0.4100	***	-0.0024	0.8481
	(2.2311)		(23.7946)		(-4.5484)		(-0.0251)	
L-S30	-0.0030		0.0342		0.4122	***	-0.0106	0.0892
	(-1.9335)		(0.6510)		(3.9470)		(-0.0915)	

The second key difference is that European low-ESG firms are only exposed to overconfidence bias, as indicated by the statistically significant FIN factor. Interestingly, the FIN factor loading for European low-ESG firms is also negative, further supporting the view that high arbitrage frictions could be a justifiable explanation.

One similarity between both regions is that the excess market return factor is statistically significant and has the largest impact on portfolio returns. However,

Table 4.5 Comparison of Regression Estimates of the Factor Model—EU vs. US

	α	*βMkt_Excess Return*		*βPEAD*		*βFIN*		R^2 Adj.
The European Union (Badía et al., 2024)								
Top 10% Portfolio	0.0002	1.034	***	−0.0141		0.0479		0.8944
Bottom 10% Portfolio	0.0035	1.041	***	−0.1652		−0.4831	***	0.7307
The United States (Author calculations)								
Top 10% Portfolio	−0.0219	0.9128	***	0.1100	***	0.1324	***	
								0.7819
Bottom 10% Portfolio	−0.0362	1.0747	***	−0.2678	***	−0.2426	***	
		0.1619		−0.3778		−0.3750		

This table shows the regression estimates of Daniel, Hirshleifer and Sun's (2020) three-factor model applied for European and US ESG leaders and laggards (Top 10% and Bottom 10%). The EU regression estimates are based on the study published by Badía, Goicoechea, and Ugarte (2024). The US regression estimates are based on author calculations. Asterisks represent statistically significant coefficients at the 0.1% (***), 1% (**) and 5% (*) significance levels

the high-ESG portfolio in the US shows less sensitivity to market reruns compared to its European counterpart. Therefore, for a sustainability-focused asset manager, investing in US high-ESG firms could offer better downside protection in times of market volatility.

Badía, Goicoechea and Ugarte (2024) do not explore the underlying reasons why ESG leaders in the EU appear to be resistant to overconfidence and limited attention biases. However, prior literature offers some insights into potential regional differences.

Ciciretti, Dalò and Ferri (2023) found that, on average, EU publicly listed firms have higher mean ESG ratings compared to their US counterparts. Their empirical study attributes this difference primarily to differences in regulatory environments and cultural factors. In the EU, stricter ESG regulations, such as Directive 2014/95/EU, mandate higher standards of sustainability disclosure, improving transparency (Ciciretti, Dalò and Ferri, 2023). This regulatory oversight likely fosters a more efficient pricing mechanism for high-ESG firms in the

EU, reducing the likelihood of behavioural mispricing. Cultural differences also play a significant role. European firms generally operate in an environment where sustainability is deeply embedded in corporate strategies (Beloe, 2016), which is likely to make high-ESG firms less prone to mispricing.

However, biases in ESG ratings add another layer of complexity. As noted by LaBella et al. (2019), there is size and region bias when it comes to ESG ratings, with larger companies and those based in Europe often receiving higher ESG ratings due to their better disclosure practices and stronger regulatory framework. Research by Drempetic, Klein, and Zwergel (2020) and Giese et al. (2019) have also identified size bias, and Doyle (2018) has confirmed the EU's regional bias. While Badía, Goicoechea, and Ugarte (2024) found that high-ESG firms in the EU are insulated from overconfidence bias and limited attention bias (lack of statistical significance), this finding may partly reflect the influence of size and region bias in ESG ratings. Moreover, recent research has shown that European ESG leaders exhibit herding behaviour (Gavrilakis and Floros, 2024). These two factors suggest that the claim that "stock prices of ESG-aware firms are more aligned with the efficient market hypothesis" (Badía, Goicoechea and Ugarte, 2024) may warrant further investigation. This presents an interesting avenue for future research as well.

4.4 Regression Estimates for Different Market Conditions (Bull and Bear Markets)

Given the dataset used in this study captures factor behaviour for nearly two decades, it reflects various market cycles in the US, including both bull and bear market phases. This long-term horizon provides an opportunity to analyze how ESG leaders and laggards are exposed to behavioural biases across different economic environments.

To distinguish between bull and bear markets, this study follows the approach used by (Badía, Goicoechea and Ugarte, 2024), which is based on the method proposed by Pagan and Sossounov (2003). Their methodology adapts concepts from business cycle analysis and applies them to equity markets, identifying sustained uptrends and downtrends through clearly defined criteria and censoring adjustments.

Accordingly, in this study, bull and bear markets were identified by locating local peaks (maximum index value) and troughs (lowest index value) within an eight-month window on both sides of a given date for the S&P 500 index. If consecutive peaks or troughs were found, only the highest peak or lowest trough was selected to ensure an alternating pattern between peaks and troughs. Afterwards, a few adjustments were made to eliminate noise. Firstly, any turning points occurring within six months from the start or end of the data series were removed. Then, peaks or troughs at the ends of the series were eliminated if they appeared too small compared to other points. Cycles that lasted less than 16 months were also removed, as they are considered too short to reflect meaningful market trends. Similarly, phases shorter than four months were excluded unless they had a significant index change of more than 20% (Pagan and Sossounov, 2003).

Table 4.5 shows the bear market phases identified in the US in 2003–2023 after following the approach proposed by Pagan and Sossounov (2003). All the other periods are considered bullish (the same approach was followed) (Table 4.6).

Table 4.6 US Bear Market Phases

Start Date	Index Value (Points)	End Date	Index Value (Points)	Change (Points)	Length of Bear Period (Days)
27-02-2004	1,144.90	31-08-2004	1,104.20	−40.70	186
31-10-2007	1,549.40	27-02-2009	735.10	−814.30	485
29-04-2011	1,363.60	30-09-2011	1,131.40	−232.20	154
29-05-2015	2,107.40	30-09-2015	1,920.00	−187.40	124
31-12-2021	4,766.20	30-09-2022	3,585.62	−1,180.58	273

This table highlights bear market periods, which are identified using the methodology outlined by Pagan and Sossounov (2003). The sample period analyzed spans from June 2005 to June 2023, with the S&P 500 index as the benchmark

The 2004 bear market was short-lived and was due to fears of a slowdown in economic growth, a change in the Federal Reserve's monetary policy (interest rates rising from four-decade lows) and crude oil price hikes. The 2007–2009 bear market was triggered by the Global Financial Crisis caused by the subprime mortgage crisis. The 2011 bear market was driven by fears of the European debt crisis and the US credit rating downgrade. The 2015 bear market was due to fears over a slowing Chinese economy and commodity price drops, which impacted global markets. Lastly, the 2022 bear market was caused by rising inflation, monetary tightening by the Federal Reserve and global economic uncertainties following the COVID-19 pandemic recovery period.

Table 4.9 shows the regression estimates for US ESG leaders and laggards under bull and bear market phases (see Table 4.7 for the regression estimates for the bull market scenario in the US, Table 4.8 for the regression estimates for the bear market scenario in the US, and Table 4.9 for the summary). Table 4.10 presents the regression estimates for EU-based ESG leaders and laggards under different market conditions (bull and bear market scenarios), as reported by Badía, Goicoechea, and Ugarte (2024).

Table 4.7 Regression Estimates of the Factor Model for the US Bull Market Scenario

	coefficient	std. error	t-ratio	p-value	
Constant (α)	−0.057	0.184	−0.310	0.757	
ESG_Dummy	−0.125	0.260	−0.479	0.632	
Market_Excess Return	1.067	0.045	23.617	1.41e-75	***
PEAD	−0.392	0.085	−4.593	6.01e-06	***
FIN	−0.221	0.056	−3.976	8.44e-05	***
ESG_Dummy * Market_Excess Return	−0.118	0.064	−1.844	0.0659	*
ESG_Dummy * PEAD	0.503	0.121	4.170	3.81e-05	***
ESG_Dummy * FIN	0.363	0.079	4.627	5.16e-06	***
R-squared	0.7847				
Adjusted R-squared	0.7806				

This table shows the regression estimates of the three-factor model from Daniel, Hirshleifer and Lin (2020) for high-ESG (Top 10%) and low-ESG (Bottom 10%) portfolios under the bull market scenario. The ESG Dummy variable takes the value of 1 for high-ESG and 0 for low-ESG portfolio returns. Asterisks represent statistically significant coefficients at the 0.1% (***), 1% (**) and 5% (*) significance levels. The full period analyzed is from June 2005 to June 2023

Both high- and low-ESG portfolios show statistically significant exposure to behavioural biases during bull markets. Interestingly, the direction of the factor loadings for PEAD and FIN remains unchanged. However, the beta coefficients of the two behavioural factors increase for both portfolios compared to the base case scenario. This suggests that behavioural biases become more pronounced during bull markets due to heightened investor optimism. Gervais and Odean (2001)

Table 4.8 Regression Estimates of the Factor Model for the US Bear Market Scenario

	coefficient	std. error	t-ratio	p-value	
Constant (α)	−0.231	0.626	−0.369	0.713	
ESG_Dummy	0.686	0.885	0.775	0.441	
Market_Excess Return	1.076	0.113	9.533	3.71e-14	***
PEAD	0.239	0.233	1.025	0.309	
FIN	−0.334	0.152	−2.198	0.031	**
ESG_Dummy * Market_Excess Return	−0.118	0.160	−0.741	0.461	
ESG_Dummy * PEAD	−0.026	0.330	−0.079	0.937	
ESG_Dummy * FIN	0.487	0.215	2.264	0.027	**
R-squared	0.7627				
Adjusted R-squared	0.7383				

This table shows the regression estimates of the three-factor model from Daniel, Hirshleifer and Lin (2020) for high-ESG (Top 10%) and low-ESG (Bottom 10%) portfolios under the bear market scenario. The ESG Dummy variable takes the value of 1 for high-ESG and 0 for low-ESG portfolio returns. Asterisks represent statistically significant coefficients at the 0.1% (***), 1% (**) and 5% (*) significance levels. The full period analyzed is from June 2005 to June 2023

and Daniel, Hirshleifer and Subrahmanyam (2001) suggest that overconfidence drives excessive trading in bull markets, with stronger effects compared to bear markets (Chuang and Lee, 2006). As investor optimism rises, investors chase past winners, further fueling price momentum and speculative behaviour.

In contrast, behavioural biases become less influential during bear markets in both portfolios. The results show that PEAD loses statistical significance in bear markets, indicating that market reactions to earnings surprises are muted during downturns. Additionally, the FIN factor shows a weakening influence, with increased p-values, suggesting that investors are less exposed to overconfidence bias in bear markets. Lower attention levels during bear markets lead to more risk aversion and less speculative behaviour as investors disengage (Hou, Peng and Xiong, 2008). This shift from optimism to risk aversion aligns with the Ostrich Effect (Karlsson, Loewenstein, and Seppi, 2009) and Prospect Theory (Kahneman

Table 4.9 Summary: Regression Estimates Under Different Market Conditions in the US (Bull and Bear Market Scenarios)

	Bull case				Bear case			
	Low ESG		High ESG		Low ESG		High ESG	
Alpha (α)	−0.0570		−0.1817		−0.2306		0.4552	
β Mkt_ Excess Return	1.0674	***	0.9495	*	1.0755	***	0.9573	
β PEAD	−0.3918	***	0.1112	***	0.2390		0.2130	
β FIN	−0.2208	***	0.1425	***	−0.3341	**	0.1526	**
Adjusted R-squared (Bull case)	0.7806							
Adjusted R-squared (Bear case)	0.7383							

This table shows the regression estimates of Daniel, Hirshleifer and Sun's (2020) three-factor model for the low-ESG (bottom 10%) and high-ESG (top 10%) portfolios in the US under bull and bear market scenarios. Asterisks represent statistically significant coefficients at the 0.1% (***), 1% (**) and 5% (*) significance levels. The full period analyzed is from June 2005 to June 2023

and Tversky, 1979), which explains how investors are more sensitive to losses and tend to focus on preserving capital during periods of uncertainty.

When examining the Market Excess Returns variable, its statistical significance in high-ESG portfolios weakens during bull markets. This suggests that investors focus more on firm-specific attributes (such as sustainability or other factors) rather than on the overall market direction. Interestingly, during bear markets, the Market Excess Returns variable loses its statistical significance in high-ESG portfolios, indicating that these portfolios offer some level of downside protection during downward markets.

EU Experience Under Different Market Conditions (Bull and Bear Markets)
According to the study by Badía, Goicoechea, and Ugarte (2024), the European high-ESG portfolio is insulated from both limited attention and overconfidence biases during both bull and bear phases (with factor loadings being statistically insignificant). The low-ESG portfolio is only exposed to overconfidence bias, which is more pronounced during the bull market than in the bear market (with higher

statistical significance in the bull market). For the regression estimates related to the EU study from Badía, Goicoechea, and Ugarte (2024), refer to Table 4.10.

Table 4.10 Regression Estimates of the Factor Model for Bull and Bear Cases (EU)

	α BEAR	α BULL	β_{Mkt} BEAR	β_{Mkt} BULL	β_{FIN} BEAR	β_{FIN} BULL	β_{PEAD} BEAR	β_{PEAD} BULL
T10	0.0023	-0.0016	1.0053 ***	1.0927 ***	0.0908	0.0131	0.1601	-0.0426
	(0.5954)	(-1.4105)	(14.1417)	(26.3568)	(0.4954)	(0.1592)	(1.3029)	(-0.5925)
B10	0.0040	0.0039	0.8972 ***	1.0345 ***	-0.9494 *	-0.3340 **	-0.5455	-0.0998
	(0.6675)	(1.8770)	(6.8974)	(10.3384)	(-2.4524)	(-2.6078)	(-1.9884)	(-0.5052)
L-S10	-0.0017	-0.0055 *	0.1082	0.0581	1.0402 *	0.3471 *	0.7056 *	0.0571 *
	(-0.2210)	(-2.3299)	(0.6127)	(0.4545)	(2.0893)	(1.9948)	(2.1325)	(0.2336)
T20	0.0035	-0.0012	1.0401 ***	1.0758 ***	0.0925	0.0248	0.0871	-0.0142
	(0.9914)	(-1.3115)	(16.9684)	(35.8520)	(0.4692)	(0.3951)	(0.6460)	(-0.2754)
B20	0.0035	0.0041 *	0.8365 ***	1.0283 ***	-0.9164 ***	-0.3519 ***	-0.2465	-0.1333
	(0.8985)	(2.5684)	(11.2859)	(15.6762)	(-4.3912)	(-3.9009)	(-1.4297)	(-1.0222)
L-S20	0.0000	-0.0053 **	0.2036	0.0474	1.0089 **	0.3767 **	0.3336	0.1192
	(0.0007)	(-3.0097)	(1.7754)	(0.5927)	(3.3947)	(3.3553)	(1.5126)	(0.7429)
T30	0.0031	-0.0006	1.0456 ***	1.0656 ***	-0.0049	0.0071	0.0437	-0.0302
	(1.0459)	(-0.7471)	(20.8133)	(42.2603)	(-0.0313)	(0.1268)	(0.4125)	(-0.6731)
B30	0.0062	0.0031 *	0.8942 ***	1.0250 ***	-0.8418 ***	-0.2382 **	-0.1179	-0.0358
	(1.5323)	(2.1076)	(13.0510)	(18.5744)	(-5.2792)	(-3.0039)	(-0.6138)	(-0.3241)
L-S30	-0.0032	-0.0037 *	0.1514	0.0406	0.8368 ***	0.2452 *	0.1615	0.0056
	(-0.6518)	(-2.2688)	(1.6467)	(0.6363)	(3.8864)	(2.2664)	(0.7055)	(0.0415)

This table shows the estimates of the three-factor model of the Daniel et al. (2020) for the top (T), bottom (B) and long-short (L-S) portfolios at the 10%, 20% and 30% cut-off level, in different market states. The long-short portfolio is formed by subtracting the returns of the bottom-ranked portfolio from the returns of the top-ranked portfolio. The model (eq. 1) is estimated by OLS based on the heteroscedasticity and autocorrelation adjusted errors of Newey and West (1987). Values in brackets are the *t*-statistics. Asterisks represent statistically significant coefficients at the 0.1% (***), 1% (**) and 5% (*) significance levels. The full period analyzed is from January 2004 to December 2022.

As mentioned in the previous section, further research may be required to determine whether the lack of statistical significance for behavioural biases among European ESG leaders is a reliable observation or a result of size and region biases in ESG ratings (LaBella et al., 2019).

4.5 Practical Implications for Stakeholders

The findings of this study have practical implications for various stakeholders.

For institutional investors, the findings show that high-ESG portfolios in the US offer better downside protection and risk mitigation, especially during volatile market conditions. These portfolios display lower sensitivity to overall market movements, suggesting that high-ESG investments may serve as a hedge against systematic risks. Additionally, the positive beta loadings on both post-earnings announcement drift (PEAD) and financing factor (FIN) in the high-ESG portfolio indicate that these portfolio returns are likely to benefit from the correction of mispricing anomalies over time.

For policymakers and regulators, the findings indicate that behavioural biases are more prevalent in the US market than in the EU, possibly due to the voluntary nature of ESG disclosures in the United States. In contrast, the mandatory

ESG reporting frameworks in the EU have led to more efficient markets. The introduction of the new sustainability standards (S1 and S2) could help bridge this gap by promoting greater transparency and comparability in ESG reporting across regions. However, the adoption of these standards is still not compulsory, and their implementation will depend on each jurisdiction's regulatory processes. This implies that there is significant potential for regulation to play a role in harmonizing ESG disclosures and mitigating regional disparities in reporting practices.

The study also provides interesting insights for equity research analysts. It shows that high-ESG portfolios exhibit low market beta, suggesting that firms in these portfolios may face a lower cost of equity due to their reduced exposure to systematic risk. Analysts can use this information to adjust their valuation models, such as by modifying the equity risk premium for high-ESG firms. Additionally, the study's findings on behavioural biases, such as the tendency for high-ESG portfolios to be less affected by biases during market downturns and the efficient correction of anomalies, can help analysts in forming their investment recommendations.

5 Limitations and Future Research

This chapter discusses several limitations of the study and suggests potential avenues for future research.

A key limitation of this study is its reliance on ESG data from a single rating provider, Refinitiv. However, ESG ratings are known to have biases related to size (Drempetic, Klein, and Zwergel, 2020; Giese et al., 2019; LaBella et al., 2019), region (Doyle, 2018; LaBella et al., 2019), and industry (LaBella et al., 2019). As a result, larger companies based in Europe often receive higher ESG ratings due to better disclosure practices and a stronger regulatory framework in the region (LaBella et al., 2019). Additionally, ESG rating schemes tend to reward companies with more disclosures. Therefore, companies can manipulate their ratings through self-reported, unaudited sustainability reports LaBella et al., 2019). Future research could address these limitations by incorporating data from multiple rating providers and considering industry-specific ESG factors.

Building on this, given the observed differences in exposure to behavioural biases among high-ESG firms in the EU and US, future studies could examine how (and/or if) cultural and regulatory differences shape behavioural biases across regions (including emerging and frontier markets as well). Additionally, investigating the impact of evolving ESG regulations and greater harmonization of sustainability standards could provide additional insights.

The differences in factor loadings between high- and low-ESG portfolios and their consistency across both bull and bear market phases present an interesting case for future research. Future studies could explore the role of arbitrage frictions in influencing factor loadings. Prior literature has used the variance of

R.M. V. Bandaranayake, *The Differential Impact of Investor Behavioural Biases on US Sustainable and Non-Sustainable Firms*, BestMasters,
https://doi.org/10.1007/978-3-658-50668-1_5

residuals from the Capital Asset Pricing Model (CAPM) regression[1] as a proxy for arbitrage costs, or in other words, firm-wide idiosyncratic risk (Wurgler and Zhuravskaya, 2002, cited in Kumar and Lee, 2006, p. 27). Arbitrage costs are generally higher for less liquid stocks; therefore, liquidity beta can also serve as an alternative proxy (Pástor and Stambaugh, 2003, cited in Kumar and Lee, 2006, p. 29). Prior studies, including Kumar and Lee (2006), confirm that arbitrage frictions are higher among stocks with lower institutional ownership, lower prices, small market capitalizations and high book-to-market ratios. The Fama-French three-factor model (1992, 1993) can be used to assess the size effect (SMB) and the low-to-high book-to-market effect (HML)[2].

Lastly, while the behavioural three-factor model demonstrates strong statistical significance for the PEAD and FIN factors, further testing reveals that much of the model's explanatory power is driven by the market factor alone (refer to Tab. 5.1). A reduced-form regression using only the market excess return yields an R^2 of 0.753, compared to 0.785 in the full model. This indicates that the behavioural factors collectively add just 3.2 percentage points of explanatory power. Additionally, the correlation between portfolio and market excess returns is as high as 0.868, highlighting the dominant role of the market factor. These findings suggest that, although PEAD and FIN offer behavioural insights, their economic significance in explaining return variation remains limited within this framework.

---

[1] Although idiosyncratic risk is a reasonable proxy for arbitrage costs, it may also represent other related factors. For instance, cited in Kumar and Lee (2006), it serves as an indicator of information uncertainty, as discussed in Jiang, Lee and Zhang (2005) and Zhang (2006). Similarly, it proxies for a stock's sensitivity to investor sentiment, as noted in Baker and Wurgler (2006).

[2] SMB (Small Minus Big) measures the difference between the returns of a portfolio composed of small stocks and a portfolio composed of large stocks, while HML (High Minus Low) reflects the difference in returns between a portfolio of high book-to-market ratio (B/M) stocks and a portfolio of low book-to-market ratio stocks (Fama and French, 1992, 1993).

Table 5.1 Regression Estimates for Standalone Market Excess Return Factor and Correlation

	coefficient	std. error	t-ratio	p-value	
Constant (α)	−0.0757	0.129	−0.5889	0.556	***
Market_Excess Return	1.016	0.028	36.370	7.78E−134	
R-squared	0.7529				
Corr (Portfolio_ExcessReturn, Market_ExcessReturn) = 0.86770841					

This table reports regression results from a single-factor model using market excess returns to explain portfolio excess returns from June 2005 to June 2023. The market factor is highly significant ($p < 0.001$) with an R^2 of 0.7529, indicating that it explains the majority of return variation. The strong correlation ($\rho = 0.8677$) between portfolio and market returns highlights the dominant role of the market factor.

Conclusion 6

This study provides insights into the role of investor behavioural biases, specifically overconfidence and limited attention, in influencing publicly quoted high- and low-ESG firms in the US. The analysis, grounded in the behavioural three-factor model introduced by Daniel, Hirshleifer, and Sun (2020), finds that these biases affect both high- and low-ESG firms to varying degrees (as indicated by positive vs. negative factor loadings).

The key findings of the study are that high-ESG firms experience more efficient price corrections, with positive loadings on both the Post-Earnings Announcement Drift (PEAD) and Financing (FIN) factors. This suggests that mispricing is corrected more quickly, leading to higher returns in the future. In contrast, low-ESG firms exhibit negative loadings on these behavioural factors, indicating persistent mispricing, likely due to high arbitrage frictions. Moreover, the study finds that behavioural biases are more pronounced during bull market phases, while in bear markets, these biases diminish, with overconfidence bias weakening and limited attention bias losing statistical significance. This suggests that high-ESG firms may offer better downside protection during market downturns, providing a strong case for their potential as safer investments in volatile times.

The study also explores regional differences. While high-ESG firms in the US are exposed to both overconfidence and limited attention biases, a European study suggests that high-ESG firms in the EU are insulated from these biases. As noted in prior literature, this could be due to stricter regulatory frameworks and enhanced sustainability disclosure requirements in the EU. These findings highlight the importance of considering regional regulatory and cultural contexts

R.M. V. Bandaranayake, *The Differential Impact of Investor Behavioural Biases on US Sustainable and Non-Sustainable Firms*, BestMasters,
https://doi.org/10.1007/978-3-658-50668-1_6

when assessing ESG investing and its relation to behavioural finance. However, this may warrant further research with robustness checks for ESG rating-related biases.

A key limitation of this study is the reliance on a single ESG data provider (Refinitiv), which may introduce biases related to size, region, and industry. Further studies could include data from multiple ESG rating providers to mitigate such biases. Future research could explore the role of arbitrage frictions in influencing factor loadings for ESG-aware firms using proxies such as residual variance from the CAPM model, liquidity beta, and the level of institutional holdings. Additionally, the study confirms that although the behavioural PEAD and FIN factors contribute statistically, their incremental explanatory power over the market factor is marginal, raising the R^2 by only 3.2 percentage points. The high correlation between portfolio and market returns highlights the dominant influence of market risk, indicating that behavioural factors' economic impact in explaining return variation is limited in this context. Future research should further investigate their role and potential enhancements.

In conclusion, this research contributes to the growing body of literature on behavioural finance and sustainable investing by highlighting how investor biases influence ESG leaders and laggards. The findings have practical implications for asset managers, regulators, and analysts seeking to better understand the complexities of ESG investing.

References

Alexander, G.J., 2000. On back-testing "zero-investment" strategies. The Journal of Business, 73(2), pp. 255–278.

Badía, G., Cortez, M.C. and Ferruz, L., 2020. Socially responsible investing worldwide: Do markets value corporate social responsibility?. Corporate Social Responsibility and Environmental Management, 27(6), pp. 2751–2764.

Badía, G., Goicoechea, E., Ugarte, J.V., 2024. Behavioural finance in sustainable finance: could socially responsible investors be more rational than conventional ones? *May 2024 version.* Available at: https://www.efmaefm.org/0EFMAMEETINGS/EFMA%20ANNUAL%20MEETINGS/2024-Lisbon/accepted%20papers/G.php [Accessed 10 January 2025].

Ball, R., Bartov, E., 1996. How naive is the stock market's use of earning information? Journal of Accounting Economics, 21(3), pp. 319–337.

Barberis, N., Shleifer, A., & Vishny, R., 1998. A model of investor sentiment. Journal of Financial Economics, 49(3), pp. 307–343.

Beal, D.J., Goyen, M. and Phillips, P., 2005. Why do we invest ethically? The Journal of Investing, 14(2), pp. 95–115.

Bernard, V., Thomas, J., 1990. Evidence that stock prices do not fully reflect the implications of current earnings for future earnings. Journal of Accounting Economics, 13(4), pp. 305–340.

Bowles, B., Reed, A.V., Ringgenberg, M.C. and Thornock, J.R., 2024. Anomaly Time. The Journal of Finance, 79(5), pp. 3543–3579.

Bradshaw, M.T., S.A. Richardson, and R.G. Sloan, 2006. The Relation between Corporate Financing Activities, Analysts' Forecasts, and Stock Returns. Journal of Accounting and Economics, 42(1–2), pp. 53–85.

Brav, A., C. Geczy, and P.A. Gompers, 2000. Is the abnormal return following equity issuances anomalous? Journal of Financial Economics, 56(2), pp. 209–249.

Brown, Stephen J. and Pope, Peter F., 1996. Post-Earnings Announcement Drift? Available at SSRN: https://ssrn.com/abstract=2587.

Carhart, M.M., 1997. On Persistence in Mutual Fund Performance. Journal of Finance, 52(1), pp. 57–82.

R.M. V. Bandaranayake, *The Differential Impact of Investor Behavioural Biases on US Sustainable and Non-Sustainable Firms*, BestMasters,
https://doi.org/10.1007/978-3-658-50668-1

Chan, L.K., Jegadeesh, N., and Lakonishok, J., 1996. Momentum strategies. The Journal of Finance, 51(5), pp. 1681–1713.

Chuang, W.I. and Lee, B.S., 2006. An empirical evaluation of the overconfidence hypothesis. Journal of Banking & Finance, 30(9), pp. 2489–2515.

Ciciretti, R., Dalò, A. and Ferri, G., 2023. Dissecting the European ESG Premium vs the US: Is It All About Non-financial Reporting?. In *Creating Value and Improving Financial Performance: Inclusive Finance and the ESG Premium* (pp. 27–57). Cham: Springer International Publishing.

Curtis, G., 2004. Modern portfolio theory and behavioral finance. The Journal of Wealth Management, 7(2), pp. 16–22.

D'Apice, V., Ferri, G. and Lipari, F., 2020. Sustainable disclosure policies and sustainable performance of European listed companies. Sustainability, 12(15), p. 5920.

Daugaard, D., 2019. Emerging new themes in environmental, social and governance investing: A systematic literature review. Accounting & Finance, 60(2), pp. 1501–1530.

Daniel, K., Hirshleifer, D. and Subrahmanyam, A., 1998. Investor psychology and security market under-and overreactions. The Journal of Finance, 53(6), pp. 1839–1885.

Daniel, K.D., Hirshleifer, D. and Subrahmanyam, A., 2001. Overconfidence, arbitrage, and equilibrium asset pricing. The Journal of Finance, 56(3), pp. 921–965.

Daniel, K., Hirshleifer, D., and Sun, L., 2020. Short-and long-horizon behavioral factors. The Review of Financial Studies, 33(4), pp. 1673–1736.

Daniel, K.D., Hirshleifer, D. & Sun, L., 2019. Short- and Long-Horizon Behavioral Factors. Review of Financial Studies, forthcoming. Available at: https://ssrn.com/abstract=3086063 [Accessed 9 January 2025].

De Bondt, W.F. and Thaler, R.H., 1995. Financial decision-making in markets and firms: A behavioral perspective. Handbooks in Operations Research and Management Science, 9, pp. 385–410.

Deegan, C., 2002. Introduction: The legitimising effect of social and environmental disclosures–a theoretical foundation. Accounting, Auditing & Accountability Journal, 15(3), pp. 282–311.

DellaVigna, S. and Pollet, J.M., 2009. Investor inattention and Friday earnings announcements. The Journal of Finance, 64(2), pp. 709–749.

Deka, J., Sharma, M., Agarwal, N. and Tiwari, K., 2023. Linking ESG-Investing Consciousness, Behavioral Biases, and Risk-Perception: Scale Validation with Specifics of Indian Retail Investors. European Journal of Business Science and Technology, 70.

Drempetic, S., Klein, C. and Zwergel, B., 2020. The influence of firm size on the ESG score: Corporate sustainability ratings under review. Journal of business ethics, 167(2), pp. 333–360.

Doyle, T.M., 2018. Ratings that don't rate: the subjective world of ESG ratings agencies. American Council for Capital Formation, pp. 65–71.

European Commission, n.d. Overview of sustainable finance. [online] European Commission. Available at: https://finance.ec.europa.eu/sustainable-finance/overview-sustainable-finance_en.

EY, 2024. Applying IFRS: Introduction to IFRS S1 and IFRS S2. Updated June 2024. Available at: https://www.ey.com/en_gl/technical/ifrs-technical-resources/introduction-to-ifrs-s1-and-ifrs-s2-updated-june-2024 [Accessed 10 Jan. 2025].

Fama, E.F., 1998. Market efficiency, long-term returns, and behavioral finance. Journal of Financial Economics, 49(3), pp. 283–306.

Fama, E.F., and French, K.R., 1992. The cross-section of expected stock returns. The Journal of Finance, 47(2), pp. 427–465.

Fama, E.F., and French, K.R., 2015. A Five-Factor Asset Pricing Model. *Journal of Financial Economics*, 116(1), pp. 1–22.

Fama, E.F., and French, K.R., 1993. Common risk factors in returns on stocks and bonds. *Journal of Financial Economics*, 33, pp. 3–56.

Foster, G., Olsen, C. and Shevlin, T., 1984. Earnings releases, anomalies, and the behavior of security returns. *Accounting Review*, pp. 574–603.

Freeman, R.E., 2010. Strategic management: A stakeholder approach. Cambridge University Press.

French, K.R., 2012. Fama/French Factors Data Library. [online] Available at: https://mba.tuck.dartmouth.edu/pages/faculty/ken.french/Data_Library/f-f_factors.html [Accessed 27 November 2024].

Gavrilakis, N. and Floros, C., 2024. Volatility and Herding Bias on ESG Leaders' Portfolios Performance. *Journal of Risk and Financial Management*, 17(2), p. 77.

Gervais, S., and T. Odean, 2001. Learning to be overconfident. *The Review of Financial Studies*, 14(1), pp. 1–27.

Giese, G., Lee, L.E., Melas, D., Nagy, Z. and Nishikawa, L., 2019. Foundations of ESG investing: How ESG affects equity valuation, risk, and performance. Journal of portfolio management, 45(5), pp. 69–83.

Griffin, J.M., Kelly, P.J. and Nardari, F., 2010. Do market efficiency measures yield correct inferences? A comparison of developed and emerging markets. *The Review of Financial Studies*, 23(8), pp. 3225–3277.

Hirshleifer, D., Lim, S.S. and Teoh, S.H., 2009. Driven to distraction: Extraneous events and underreaction to earnings news. *The Journal of Finance*, 64(5), pp. 2289–2325.

Hirshleifer, D. and Jiang, D., 2010. A financing-based misvaluation factor and the cross-section of expected returns. *The Review of Financial Studies*, 23(9), pp. 3401–3436.

Hörisch, J., Freeman, R.E., & Schaltegger, S., 2014. Applying Stakeholder Theory in Sustainability Management: Links, Similarities, Dissimilarities, and a Conceptual Framework. *Organization & Environment*, 27(4), pp. 328–346. https://doi.org/10.1177/1086026614535786

Hou, K., Peng, L. and Xiong, W., 2009. A tale of two anomalies: The implications of investor attention for price and earnings momentum. Available at SSRN 976394.

Hung, M., Li, X., Wang, S., 2015. Post-earnings-announcement drift in global markets: Evidence from an information shock. *Review of Financial Studies*, 28(4), pp. 1242–1283.

Ikenberry, D., J. Lakonishok, and T. Vermaelen, 1995. Market underreaction to open market share repurchases. *Journal of Financial Economics*, 39(2–3), pp. 181–208.

Jiang, Guohua, Charles M.C. Lee, and Yi Zhang, 2005. Information uncertainty and expected returns. *Review of Accounting Studies*, 10, pp. 185–221.

Kahneman, D., 1979. Prospect theory: An analysis of decisions under risk. *Econometrica*, 47, pp. 278–320.

Karlsson, N., Loewenstein, G., and Seppi, D., 2009. The ostrich effect: Selective attention to information. *Journal of Risk and Uncertainty*, 38(2), pp. 95–115.

Kumar, A. and Lee, C.M., 2006. Retail investor sentiment and return comovements. *The Journal of Finance*, 61(5), pp. 2451–2486.

Lakonishok, J., and T. Vermaelen, 1990. Anomalous Price Behavior Around Repurchase Tender Offers. *Journal of Finance*, 45(2), pp. 455–477.

LaBella, M.J., Sullivan, L., Russell, J. and Novikov, D., 2019. The Devil is in the Details: The Divergence in ESG Data and Implications for Sustainable Investing. QS Investors. Available at: https://qsinvestorsproduction.blob.core.windows.net/media/Default/PDF/The%20Devil%20is%20in%20the%20Details_Divergence%20in%20ESG%20Data.pdf [Accessed 27 December 2024].

Loughran, T., and J. R. Ritter, 1995. The new issues puzzle. *Journal of Finance*, 50(1), pp. 23–51.

Loughran, T., and J. R. Ritter, 2000. Uniformly least powerful tests of market efficiency. *Journal of Financial Economics*, 55(3), pp. 361–389.

Michailova, J. and Schmidt, U., 2016. Overconfidence and bubbles in experimental asset markets. *Journal of Behavioral Finance*, 17(3), pp. 280–292.

Mullainathan, S. and Thaler, R.H., 2000. Behavioral Economics. National Bureau of Economic Research Working Paper Series, No. 7948. Available at: http://www.nber.org/papers/w7948 [Accessed 05 January 2025].

Myers, S.C. and N.S. Majluf, 1984. Corporate Financing and Investment Decisions when Firms Have Information That Investors do not Have. *Journal of Financial Economics*, 13(2), pp. 187–221.

Nofsinger, J. and Varma, A., 2014. Socially responsible funds and market crises. *Journal of Banking & Finance*, 48, pp. 180–193.

Nilsson, J., 2009. Segmenting socially responsible mutual fund investors: The influence of financial return and social responsibility. *International Journal of Bank Marketing*, 27(1), pp. 5–31.

Novy-Marx, R., 2013. The other side of value: The gross profitability premium. *Journal of Financial Economics*, 108(1), pp. 1–28.

Pontiff, J., and A. Woodgate, 2008. Share Issuance and Cross-Sectional Returns. *The Journal of Finance*, 63(2), pp. 921–945.

Pástor, Ľ. and Stambaugh, R.F., 2003. Liquidity risk and expected stock returns. *Journal of Political Economy*, 111(3), pp. 642–685.

Pratama, A., Dewi, N., Sofia, P., Muhammad, K. and Megawati, L.R., 2024. Sustainability Reporting Ecosystem and IFRS S1 and S2: How Accounting Research can assist its Implementation. *Journal of Ecohumanism*, 3(4), pp. 3101–3129.

Renneboog, L., Ter Horst, J., and Zhang, C., 2006. Is ethical money financially smart?. *ECGI-Finance Working Paper*, (117).

Rooh, S., El-Gohary, H., Khan, I., Alam, S., and Shah, S.M.A., 2023. An attempt to understand stock market investors' behaviour: The case of environmental, social, and governance (ESG) forces in the Pakistani stock market. *Journal of Risk and Financial Management*, 16(12), p. 500.

Rubbaniy, Ghulame, Shoaib Ali, Costas Siriopoulos, and Aristeidis Samitas. 2021. Global Financial Crisis, COVID-19, Lockdown, and Herd Behavior in the US ESG Leader Stocks. Available at SSRN: https://ssrn.com/abstract=3868114 [Accessed 8 January 2025].

Shiller, R.J., 2003. From efficient markets theory to behavioral finance. *Journal of Economic Perspectives*, 17(1), pp. 83–104.

Shiller, R.J., 2006. Tools for financial innovation: Neoclassical versus behavioral finance. *Financial Review*, 41(1), pp. 1–8.

Scott, J., Stumpp, M. and Xu, P., 2003. Overconfidence bias in international stock prices. *The Journal of Portfolio Management*, 29(2), pp. 80–89.

Skrivanek, S., 2009. The Use of Dummy Variables in Regression Analysis. Available at: https://www.moresteam.com/WhitePapers/download/dummy-variables.pdf [Accessed 28 November 2024].

Statman, M., 1995. Behavioral finance versus standard finance. In *AIMR Conference Proceedings* (Vol. 7, pp. 14–22). CFA Institute.

Stein, J.C., 1996. Rational Capital Budgeting in an Irrational World. *Journal of Business*, 69(4), pp. 429–455.

Suchman, M.C., 1995. Managing legitimacy: Strategic and institutional approaches. *The Academy of Management Review*, 20(3), pp. 571–610.

Sun, L., 2023. FIN and PEAD factor returns (1972:07–2023:12) [Monthly] [Daily]. Available at: DHS factors monthly 1972–2023.xlsx [Accessed 18 December 2024].

Thaler, R.H., 1980. Toward a positive theory of consumer choice. *Journal of Economic Behavior & Organization*, 1(1), pp. 39–60.

Thaler, R.H., 1999. The end of behavioral finance. *Financial Analysts Journal*, 55(6), pp. 12–17.

The Nobel Prize, 2013. The Nobel Prize. [Online]. Available at: https://www.nobelprize.org/prizes/economic-sciences/2013/popular-information/#:~:text=These%20findings%2C%20which%20may%20seem,Peter%20Hansen%20and%20Robert%20Shiller.

Thomson Reuters, 2018. Thomson Reuters ESG Scores: Methodology. [pdf] Available at: https://www.researchgate.net/profile/Bita_Mashayekhi/post/ESG_Ratings-Are_there_any_ESG_ratings_that_require_particiaption_in_order_to_be_listed/attachment/5e69de1fcfe4a7bbe5652a52/AS:868158177046528@1583996447761/download/esg-scores-methodology.pdf [Accessed 07 November 2024].

Wang, X.W., Yan, Z., Zhang, Q. and Gao, X., 2017. Investor attention and stock market under-reaction to earnings announcements: Evidence from the options market. *The Journal of Futures Markets*, 38(4), pp. 478–492.

Wurgler, J. and Zhuravskaya, E., 2002. Does arbitrage flatten demand curves for stocks?. *The Journal of Business*, 75(4), pp. 583–608.

Zhang, X. Frank, 2006. Information uncertainty and stock returns. *Journal of Finance*, 61, pp. 105–137.

MIX
Papier aus verantwortungsvollen Quellen
Paper from responsible sources
FSC® C105338

If you have any concerns about our products,
you can contact us on
ProductSafety@springernature.com

In case Publisher is established outside the EU,
the EU authorized representative is:
Springer Nature Customer Service Center GmbH
Europaplatz 3, 69115 Heidelberg, Germany

Printed by Libri Plureos GmbH
in Hamburg, Germany